CoolBrands® 2009/10

An insight into some of Britain's coolest brands

CoolBrands®
2009/10

Chief Executive	Managing Editor	Brand Liaison Directors	Brand Liaison Manager	Head of Accounts
Ben Hudson	**Angela Cooper**	**Fiona Maxwell** **Liz Silvester**	**Heidi Smith**	**Will Carnochan**

Publishing Agency
August Media
augustmedia.com

Creative and Production
Agency, CoolBrands® digital
FMG
wearefmg.com

Published by
Superbrands (UK) Ltd.
22-23 Little Portland Street
London W1W 8BU

Prepress by Zebra
Printed in Italy
ISBN: 978-0-9554784-8-2

Mixed Sources
Product group from well-managed forests and other controlled sources
www.fsc.org Cert no. CQ-COC-000012
© 1996 Forest Stewardship Council
FSC

Foreword

Katrina Larkin

Co-Founder, The Big Chill and CoolBrands®
Expert Council Member

More than ever, in our rapidly changing, increasingly media-savvy world, we're altering the way in which we make decisions about what constitutes cool. Broadcast media no longer has a stranglehold on our attentions and the internet, in all its forms, fragments opinion and spreads alternative views. It's harder than ever to see what's coming next in this arena; people are deciding what's cool and what's not via their own networks. Personally, I think that's making what's cool more exciting than ever.

I hope this selection of brands provides a healthy platform for debate out there.

12 About CoolBrands®
14 The Selection Process
16 The Brands

Agent Provocateur
Alexander McQueen
Apple
Aston Martin
Aveda
BBC iPlayer
Belvedere Vodka
Bisque
Burberry
Burton
Busaba Eathai
Cobra
Dave
Dazed & Confused
Dermalogica
Design Museum

Disaronno
DOLCE V
Dom Pérignon
Evian
Farrow & Ball
Fever-Tree
first direct
Gaydar.co.uk
Georgina Goodman
Gio-Goi
Globe-Trotter
Grolsch
Hakkasan
Harley-Davidson
Harman Kardon
ICA
James Brown London
Jelly Belly®
KEF
Kéraskin Esthetics

Kérastase
KETTLE® Chips
Kiss
Last.fm
Leatherman®
LG
Mr & Mrs Smith
nails inc.
Olympus
Orange
PlayStation®
Poggenpohl
Pret A Manger
Proud Galleries
Ray-Ban
Roberts Radio
Rough Trade Shops
Roundhouse
Russian Standard Vodka
Sanderson

Skype
St Martins Lane
St. Tropez
Stella Artois
Storm
Tanqueray gin
The Cinnamon Club
The Glenlivet
The Zetter
Virgin Atlantic
Wahaca
Yauatcha
YouTube

156 Expert Council 2009/10
170 CoolBrands® Book
172 CoolBrands® digital
174 Qualifying CoolBrands® 2009/10

About CoolBrands®

CoolBrands® is an annual initiative to identify and pay tribute to the nation's coolest brands. Since 2001, we have been canvassing the opinions of experts and consumers to produce a yearly barometer of the coolest brands, people and places in Britain.

In addition to this book, the 2009/10 CoolBrands are celebrated online via CoolBrands digital and in print via our national media supplement. Each brand featured in this, the eighth annual programme, has qualified for inclusion based on the collective opinions of the independent and voluntary Expert Council and more than 2,500 people from across Britain. Further details of the selection process are provided overleaf.

The annual CoolBrands programme is administered by Superbrands (UK) Ltd. Superbrands was launched in London in 1995 and is now a global business operating in more than 55 countries.

The Selection Process

Each year just 500 CoolBrands® are chosen by the Expert Council and members of the British public. Brands do not pay or apply to be considered. The entire selection process is independently administered by The Centre for Brand Analysis – visit tcba.co.uk for full details.

The 2009/10 Expert Council

Walé Adeyemi	Fashion Designer
Simon Armstrong	Head of Retail, Design Museum
Niku Banaie	Managing Director, Isobar Global
Damian Barr	Journalist, Writer, Playwright & Presenter
Ed Bartlam	Co-Founder & Director, Underbelly Ltd
Edith Bowman	Radio & TV Broadcaster
Kevin Braddock	Contributing Editor, GQ
Patrick Burgoyne	Editor, Creative Review
Neil Byrne	Board Director, Camron
Kate Creasey	Editor, Cosmopolitan.co.uk
Sarah J Edwards	Director, BLAG UK Ltd
Lee Farrant	Partner, RPM Group
Sadie Frost	Actress & Fashion Designer
Sandra Halliday	Global Managing Editor, Real-Time Reporting & Analysis, WGSN
Newby Hands	Associate Editor & Director of Health & Beauty, Harper's Bazaar
Andrew Harrison	Associate Editor, The Word & Editor-in-Chief, Mixmag
Jack Horner	Co-Founder & Creative Director, FRUKT
Lucy Johnston	Brand Innovation Consultant/ Founder, The Neon Birdcage
Dolly Jones	Editor, VOGUE.COM

Katrina Larkin	Co-Founder, The Big Chill
Ben de Lisi	Fashion Designer
Kay McMahon	Digital Director, Wallpaper*
James Murphy	Founding Partner, adam & eve
Trevor Nelson	DJ
Steve Parkinson	Managing Director, London Radio, Bauer Media
Lauretta Roberts	Digital Development Director, WGSN
Nicolas Roope	Founding Partner, Poke London
Tom Savigar	Partner, The Future Laboratory
Jess Search	Chief Executive, Channel 4 BRITDOC Foundation
Stuart Semple	Artist
Michael Acton Smith	CEO, Mind Candy
Roger Wade	Director, Brands Incorporated
Stephen Cheliotis	Chairman, Superbrands Councils UK & Chief Executive, The Centre for Brand Analysis

Turn to p156 for more about the Expert Council

The Brands

Agent Provocateur

As Agent Provocateur enters its 15th anniversary year, the luxury lingerie brand is stronger and more seductive than ever

Agent Provocateur's 2009/10 campaign 'The New World Order' further confirms why it is renowned as the world's most fashion-forward and imaginative lingerie brand. A phenomenal success story with 44 stores worldwide and a thriving fragrance business, Agent Provocateur is a truly credible lingerie brand, which is committed to investment in creativity led by pure instinct of that which is beautiful and of course erotic. Knickers Forever!

Agent Provocateur

agentprovocateur.com

Alexander McQueen

A mix of bespoke British tailoring, the fine workmanship of the French haute couture atelier and the impeccable finish of Italian manufacturing creates Alexander McQueen's signature look

London-born Alexander McQueen is known both for the emotional power and raw energy of his shows, and the romantic but determinedly contemporary nature of his collections. Integral to the McQueen culture is the juxtaposition of contrasting elements: fragility and strength, tradition and modernity, fluidity and severity. He is also influenced by the arts and crafts tradition for which he has a profound respect.

ALEXANDER
MQUEEN

alexandermcqueen.com

Apple

Sleek, stylish design combined with powerful, groundbreaking technology make Apple's unique products iconic must-haves around the world

Apple has been challenging the status quo for over 30 years. It ignited the personal-computer revolution in the 1970s with the Apple II, reinvented computers in the 1980s with the Macintosh, and continues to lead the industry today with its innovative, award-winning designs. The brand is spearheading the digital media revolution with its portable iPods, online iTunes store and revolutionary iPhone. Small wonder, then, that Apple topped Fortune magazine's World's 50 Most Admired Companies list in 2009.

apple.com

Aston Martin

Sleek design, with perfectly proportioned bodywork, luxury interiors and impeccable attention to detail – an Aston Martin combines power and sporting ability with refinement and beauty

A strong racing heritage and exceptional quality and craftsmanship have kept Aston Martin at the forefront of car manufacturing and racing for 95 years. Founded in 1914 by Lionel Martin and Robert Bamford, Aston Martin built sports cars with a distinctive and individual character, to the highest standards and exceeding all performance expectations. The brand has stayed true to these values, creating some of the most iconic British sports cars of the post-war era, ranging from the DB5 driven by 007 in Goldfinger to, most recently, Aston Martin's definitive sports car, the stunning One-77.

astonmartin.com

Aveda

The growing range of Aveda's botanically based professional haircare and skincare products sums up its core philosophy – to set an example for environmental leadership and responsibility

Not only does Aveda use 100% wind power in its manufacturing but it's also one of the largest purchasers of organic ingredients in the personal care industry and sets a benchmark for environmental packaging. As well as raising over $14 million for Earth Month and winning PETA's Best Cruelty-Free Spa Products Proggy Award 2008, Aveda is the first beauty company to receive a Cradle to Cradle sustainability endorsement. Fashion-focused, it has created catwalk looks at New York and London Fashion Weeks and has styled many famous faces, including the stars of Slumdog Millionaire.

aveda.co.uk

BBC iPlayer

Since Christmas 2007, BBC iPlayer has been 'making the unmissable unmissable' by giving audiences access to BBC TV and radio programmes from the past seven days

BBC iPlayer offers viewers in the UK the chance to catch up on more than 400 hours of BBC programming and has quickly established itself as the nation's favourite catch-up service, with nearly 500 million total TV streams since launch. It is simple to use and now available on a range of electronic devices such as mobile phones, TV services, games consoles and media players as well as via the internet.

bbc.co.uk/iplayer

Belvedere Vodka

Hailing from a century-old distillery in the town of Żyrardów in Poland, Belvedere, the world's first super-premium vodka, was named after the presidential palace of its homeland

Following traditions dating back over 600 years, Belvedere is handcrafted in small batches exclusively using Dankowskie Gold rye to ensure superior quality. Completely free of artificial flavours and additives, Belvedere is distilled four times, the optimum number for enhancing its subtle sweetness and smooth finish, and blended with water from the distillery's artesian wells. Also available, Belvedere Citrus, Belvedere Orange and Belvedere Black Raspberry are all flavoured using a 100% natural maceration process, which is unique to the brand.

belvedere-vodka.com

BELVEDERE
VODKA

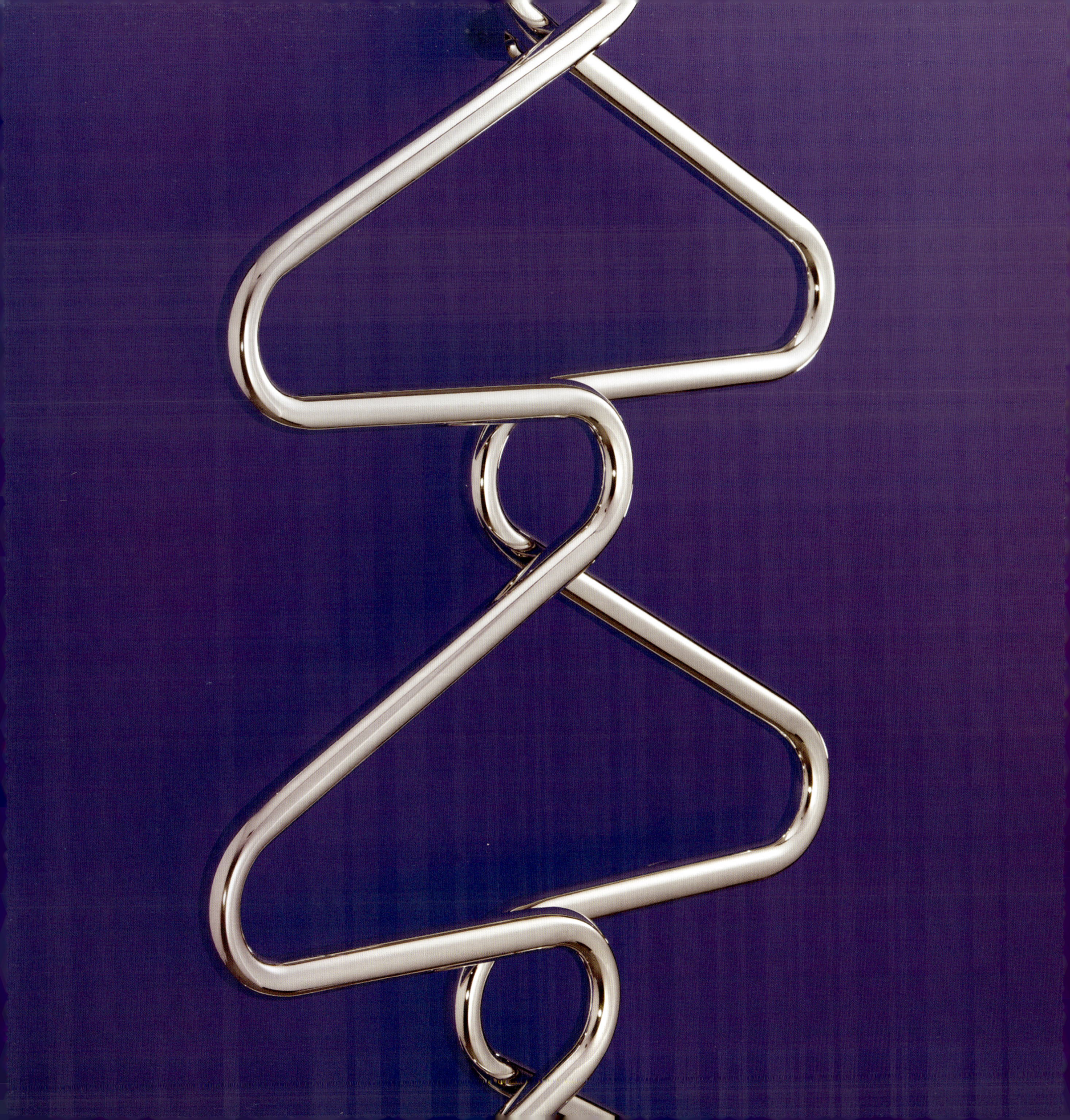

Bisque

Market-leading radiator company Bisque is 30 years old this year. Innovative, uncompromising design, superb quality and excellent service have kept it at the forefront of interior design

Bisque started as a small London plumbing company and went on to revolutionise the radiator market with exciting, sculptural designs that combined wow factor and performance. Today, Bisque continues to innovate, with cutting-edge designs commissioned from both top product designers and new, young talent. Bisque has won creative awards worldwide and its passion to be the best means excellent service, technical expertise and attention to detail as well as an unrivalled choice of styles and finishes.

BISQUE

bisque.co.uk

Burberry

Burberry is an iconic global luxury brand with a worldwide distribution network. It stands for quality, innovation, style and dishevelled elegance – always with a distinctly British attitude

The Burberry brand, founded in 1856, is anchored in the integrity of its outerwear, a tradition that began when Thomas Burberry invented gabardine. The Burberry trench coat has become renowned for its functionality as much as for its elegance. This signature style is also seen in men's and women's outerwear, ready-to-wear and accessories collections, which are naturally influenced by a rich heritage of over 150 years. Burberry recently moved to new global headquarters at Horseferry House in London and also has offices on Madison Avenue in New York.

BURBERRY

burberry.com

Burton

Rider-driven and dedicated purely to creating the best snowboarding equipment on Earth, Burton Snowboards continues to break the boundaries of snowboarding innovation in its 32nd year

In 1977, Jake Burton Carpenter founded Burton Snowboards out of his Vermont barn. Since then, Burton has fuelled the growth of snowboarding worldwide through its groundbreaking product lines, its team of top snowboarders and its grassroots efforts to get the sport accepted at resorts. In 1996, Burton began growing its family of brands to include boardsports and apparel. Privately held and owned by Jake, Burton's headquarters are in Burlington, Vermont with offices in California, Austria, Japan and Australia.

burton.com

Busaba Eathai

Conceived by Alan Yau, Busaba Eathai arrived in Wardour Street, London, in 1999 as a modern interpretation of the traditional authentic Thai canteen

Inspired by the social dynamics of sharing dishes around a large, square communal table, Busaba Eathai echoes this informal approach to dining. Interior designer Christian Liaigre has brought a tranquil backdrop to the experience of group eating, using warm and tactile materials such as teak, bronze and slate. Offering traditional Thai classics, the menu is ever-evolving, as is Busaba Eathai itself, using regional Thai influences for new direction. Three branches can now be found in London, with plans for more restaurants around the UK in the next five years.

busaba.com

Cobra

Cobra is specifically brewed to a traditional Indian recipe to be smooth and less bloating, making it the ideal accompaniment to spicy, exotic food

First brewed in Bangalore in 1989, Cobra was initially sold direct to Indian restaurants. Today you will find Cobra in almost every supermarket and licensed Indian restaurant, in thousands of pubs and in over 50 countries worldwide. At Cobra's heart is an obsession with quality, resulting in a plethora of brewing awards; a commitment to social responsibility, spawning independent charity, The Cobra Foundation; and a pride in its roots, inspiring the iconography on Cobra's bottles, depicting the brand's unique and colourful story.

cobrabeer.com

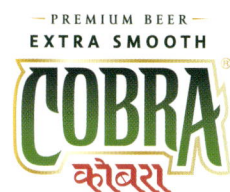

Dave

The world of Dave is designed to emulate a stately gentlemen's club where (like its programming) unexpected things happen. Rich visual ephemera create a unique, adventurous brand

At Dave's heart is intelligent, irreverent humour – content that satisfies the male need for banter with other men. For fans, it's not a TV channel but a surrogate pub – only here, they're mates with Stephen Fry, Jack Dee and Jeremy Clarkson. Dave has become commissioner extraordinaire, attracting the highest ever ratings for a non-terrestrial channel (2.68 million) by reuniting the cast of Red Dwarf. The brand's ambition is to extend beyond its televisual beginnings.

Dave
the home of witty banter

joindave.co.uk

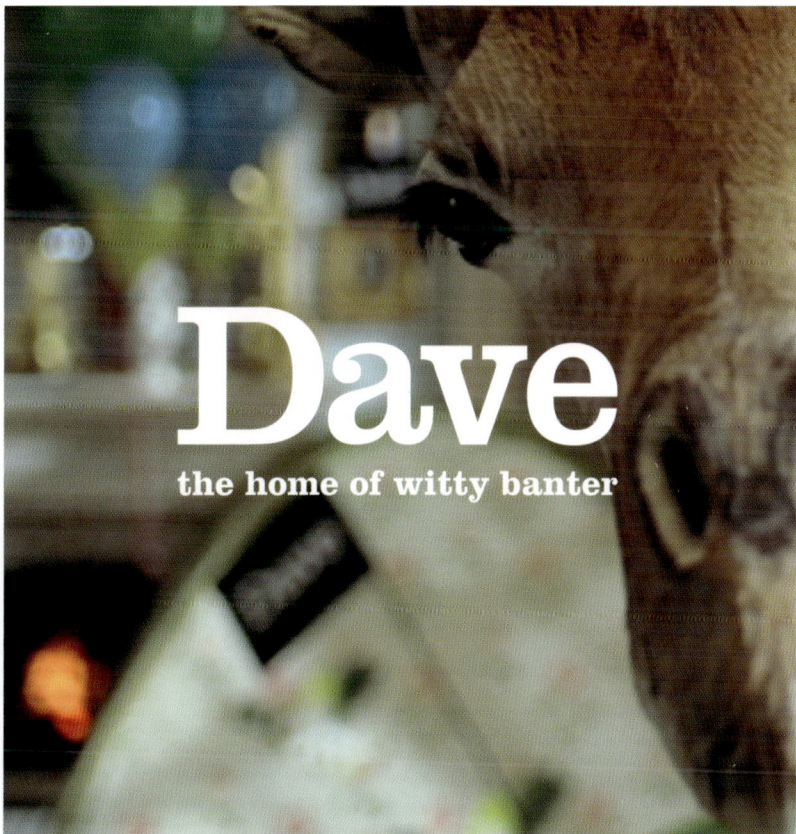

DAZED &CONFUSED

THE MAVERICKS ISSUE WITH BETH DITTO, WERNER HERZOG, PEACHES & MORE

THE UNSTOPPABLE RISE OF THE GOSSIP

KISS THIS!

Dazed & Confused

A trailblazer for emerging talent and proudly independent, Dazed & Confused magazine aims to set the cultural agenda, both on and offline

Founded by Jefferson Hack and Rankin, Dazed & Confused is a 100% independent British fashion, culture and arts magazine, which began life as a fold-out 'zine in 1992. It now has a strong global reputation for its groundbreaking and trendsetting editorial and its support of the next generation of talent in the worlds of fashion, art, literature, photography and music. Meanwhile, DazedDigital.com is updated daily and plays host to interactive projects, exclusive music, and fashion films.

DAZED & CONFUSED

dazeddigital.com

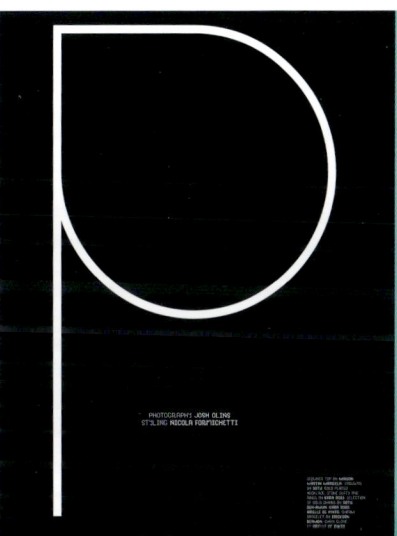

Dermalogica

Recommended by skincare professionals worldwide, Dermalogica's innovative and educational approach to skin health delivers proven results without frilly packaging or hype

Available exclusively by professional recommendation, Dermalogica's simple, modern products are infused with some of the best ingredients science and nature can provide. Key to the brand's success is that it delivers results without the overblown claims and glamorous trappings often associated with skincare. A true pioneer in the industry, Dermalogica is driven by its belief in education and research, staying true to its founding vision of skin health.

dermalogica

dermalogica.com

Hussein Chalayan, Temporal
Meditations SS 2004.

Design Museum

London's Design Museum is one of the world's leading institutions devoted to contemporary design in every guise, from furniture to graphics, and architecture to industrial design

Described by the Financial Times as 'the premier advocate and judge of good design in the UK', the Design Museum is shaping the public's appreciation and understanding of design and architecture. Through its exhibitions, educational programme, collections, online presence and publishing projects, it aims to provide a critical insight into the creative forces driving change in today's world. An institution with international status and significance, the Design Museum plays a vital role in making design and architecture a part of the cultural agenda.

DESIGN MUSEUM

designmuseum.org

Luke Hayes/Mariscal – Drawing Life Timothy Davey

Disaronno

Created in 1525 as a token of love, by a Saronno innkeeper for her artist lover, Disaronno is still made to the original secret recipe and remains the world's favourite Italian liqueur

As well as its unique bottle design, Disaronno is recognised for its warm and distinctive taste – unchanged since its creation during the Renaissance. On its own, over ice, or in cocktails such as the classic Amaretto sour, the liqueur's rich Italian heritage is unmistakable. Disaronno has secured a following of stylish young women by cultivating sponsorship and celebrity links within the arena of fashion and style. Recent associations have included Vivienne Westwood and accessory designers Antoni & Alison.

disaronno.co.uk

DISARONNO®

DOLCE V

The philosophy of DOLCE V is to offer a carefully edited selection of high-quality, original lingerie labels from innovators and specialists around the world

DOLCE V is an online lingerie and beachwear boutique founded by Italian-born Lucia Mizzoni. It has a constantly evolving collection of specialist brands such as Chantelle, Cosabella, Damaris, Mimi Holliday and Spanx. DOLCE V takes pride in introducing designers and labels available exclusively on the site, such as the Italian brand Adorisadora. The site also contains features such as an interactive bra-measuring tool to help customers achieve the perfect fit.

dolcev.com

Opposite: Margherita Mazzei – DOLCE V Exclusive
This page: Patrizia Pepe – DOLCE V Exclusive

Dom Pérignon

From the 17th-century court of Louis XIV to the company of contemporary influencers, Dom Pérignon has always lived in the world of luxury

In 1668 a young monk, Dom Pérignon, was appointed cellar master of the Benedictine Abbey of Hautvillers in the western hills of France. He made it his mission to create the best wine in the world and in his quest for perfection became renowned as the spiritual father of champagne. Each Dom Pérignon vintage is a renewed creation and ages for a minimum of seven years to reach its unmistakable style. A star amongst stars, it has seduced real-life and fictional icons from Marilyn Monroe to James Bond, as well as modern influencers such as Marc Newson and Karl Lagerfeld.

domperignon.com

Evian

Born in the pristine peaks of the French Alps, Evian is one of the world's most iconic brands and has long-standing associations with the world of glamour

Evian has long been associated with French style, glamour and sophistication. From annual collaborations with some of the world's best-known fashion designers (including Christian Lacroix and Jean Paul Gaultier), to its long-established involvement with London Fashion Week, Evian is equally at home on the catwalk as it is in the Alps. Since 2008 it has been an official sponsor of the world's most famous tennis tournament, Wimbledon, bringing French chic to south west London.

evian.com

Farrow & Ball

Farrow & Ball paints and wallpapers have been traditionally made in Dorset since 1946 and are renowned throughout the world for their depth and beauty of colour

Farrow & Ball is one of the only companies that manufactures a range of both traditional and modern paint finishes of the highest quality, in a palette of 132 unrivalled colours. A dedication to using high-quality natural ingredients means that its eco-friendly paints contain low or minimal VOCs (Volatile Organic Compounds). The same is true of Farrow & Ball's wallpaper: nobody else uses their own water-based paints and traditional printing methods to create environmentally friendly wallpapers of exceptional texture and beauty, which are quite simply unique.

farrow-ball.com

FARROW & BALL
Manufacturers of Traditional Papers and Paint

Fever-Tree

Pioneering a new drinks category worldwide, Fever-Tree's award-winning range of premium natural mixers has changed the perception of the mixer forever

Fever-Tree's premium natural mixers evolved from a desire to enhance the quality of long drinks. By replacing saccharin sweeteners and artificial preservatives with natural botanicals and flavours, they created delicious mixers that complement the finest spirits. Acclaimed by gastronomes worldwide, Fever-Tree mixers are sold in 15 countries and stocked in six of the world's top 10 restaurants (selected by Restaurant Magazine). Innovative product launches continue to increase drinkers' choice. After all, if two-thirds of your long drink is the mixer, that mixer had better be good.

fever-tree.com

Every penny is beautiful

first direct

Making banking easy, treating customers with respect and understanding that their time is precious are what first direct is all about. Its aim has always been to put customers' needs first

When it launched in 1989, first direct broke the traditional banking mould by being telephone-based with no branches. Twenty years on, the web plays an important role in maintaining its straightforward banking principles but having real people for customers to talk to 24/7/365 is still key. The original concept of really understanding customers and trying to save them time lives on, through the philosophy of providing easy access, convenience, security and flexibility.

first direct

firstdirect.com

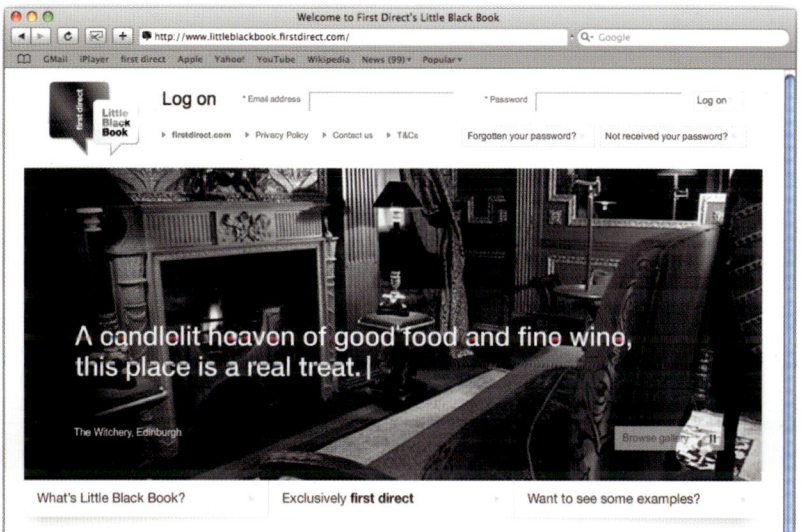

Gaydar.co.uk

The way that gay people meet across the world has been revolutionised by Gaydar.co.uk. Now the world's largest gay brand, Gaydar is celebrating 10 years of bringing people together

Gaydar is the busiest gay dating website in the world. It launched with the aim of being less formal and easier to use than the competition and grew through word of mouth. More than five million men now have Gaydar profiles, which they exchange as regularly as phone numbers. For thousands of isolated individuals who live in countries where homosexuality remains illegal, or homophobia highly prevalent, this community is an invaluable lifeline that allows them to chat freely, confidentially and safely with like-minded people.

gaydar.co.uk

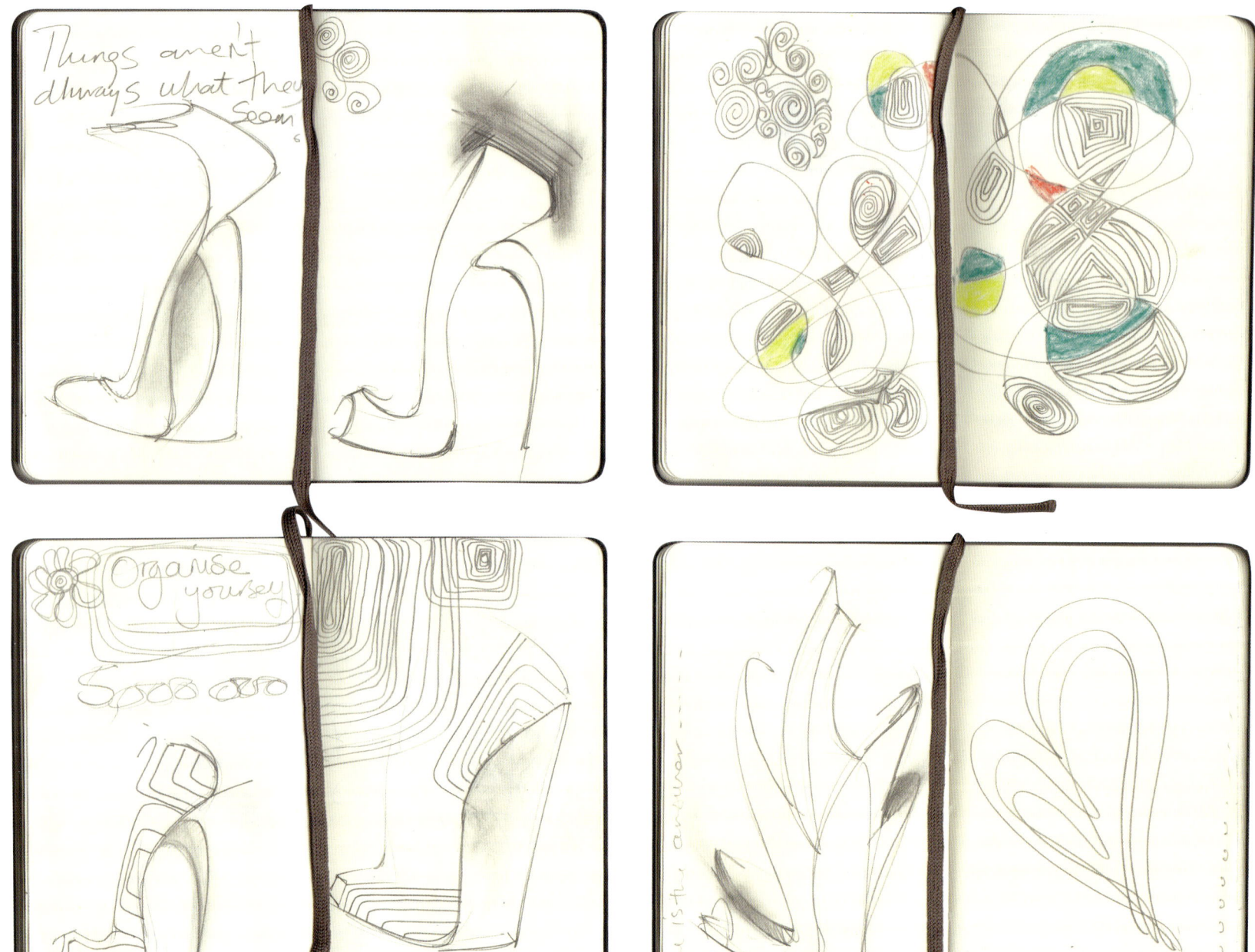

Georgina Goodman

The understated luxury expressed in the consistent signature style of Georgina Goodman's shoe collections has sealed her position as 'the designer's shoe designer'

Georgina Goodman's brand philosophy is: 'Be consistent, be clear, be who we really are and most importantly, be in love'. This is expressed in all things Georgina Goodman, down to placing the words 'Made in love' on the hand-painted, striped sole of every shoe. Handmade in Italy, her directional, contemporary collections can be found in the world's leading fashion retailers and through her flagship store on London's prestigious Old Bond Street.

GEORGINA GOODMAN

georginagoodman.com

Made in love x

Gio-Goi

Founded in 1988, Gio-Goi emerged from the dance revolution that swept over Britain during the late 80s and early 90s

Now in its 21st anniversary year, this unorthodox fashion brand still captures the excitement and progressive attitude of the second 'Summer of Love'. In darkened warehouses, under the lasers of the super clubs and beneath the stars of the best festivals, the label is embraced by everyone from clubbers through to the DJs, artists and bands that keep the essence of Gio-Goi real. With its fusion of music and fashion, the Gio-Goi tour bus travels around the UK's festivals and music events, while also partying alongside world-famous DJs and an army of dedicated clubbers in Ibiza. The journey continues.

gio-goi.com

Globe-Trotter

Handmade in England since 1897, the Globe-Trotter suitcase remains a great British icon in the world of luxury travel. A truly covetable, modern-day masterpiece

Synonymous with great British design, Globe-Trotter could be described as the definition of Handmade Luxury Luggage. Established in 1897 and crafted from vulcanised fibreboard with English leather trim, Globe-Trotter suitcases offer a uniquely strong yet lightweight functionality with a stark, instantly recognisable aesthetic. One of the world's most loved and sought-after suitcases, Globe-Trotter has been the luggage choice of iconic British figures, past and present, from Sir Winston Churchill to Daniel Craig, and Queen Elizabeth II to Kate Moss.

globe-trotterltd.com

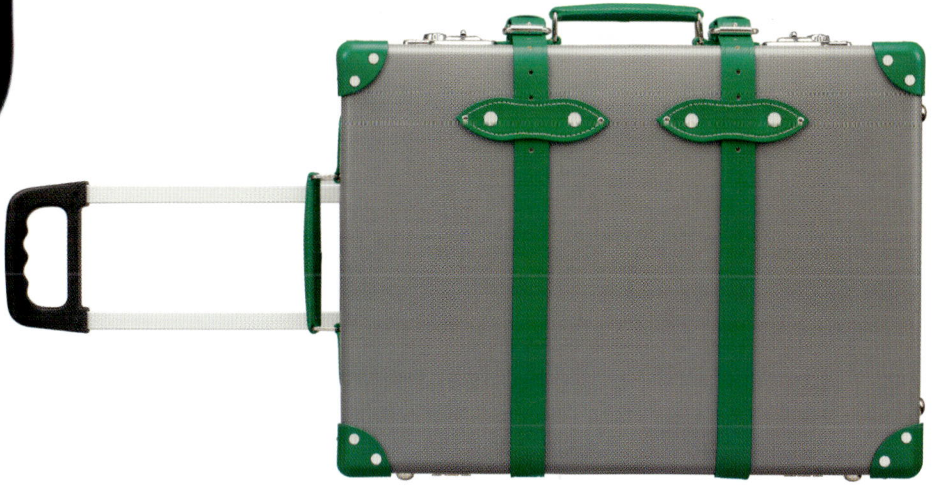

Grolsch

Slow-brewed in Holland since 1615, it's Grolsch's special extra ingredient – time – that marks it out as a classic, spicy and refreshing premium Dutch lager

Grolsch's unique flavour is derived solely from four natural ingredients – 100% malted barley, mineral water, a double dose of carefully blended taste-and-aroma hops and Grolsch's secret strain of yeast. So secret in fact that it's guarded in secure vaults in three cities. The results, however, can be found and enjoyed in bars around the world, instantly recognisable by the iconic, green swing-top bottle.

grolsch.co.uk

Hakkasan

In 2001 Alan Yau opened Hakkasan in London's Fitzrovia. Two years later it was awarded a Michelin star

From its inception, Hakkasan has been recognised for the quality of its interior design as well as the quality of its food. The work of renowned interior designer Christian Liaigre, its modern interior retains a distinctively Asian feel. Meanwhile, the dedication to the art of Chinese cuisine shown by head chef Tong Chee Hwee has seen Hakkasan achieve many culinary awards, including the number one position within Time Out magazine's Top 50 Restaurants in London listing in 2008.

hakkasan.com

Harley-Davidson

With over 100 years of American design heritage, a Harley-Davidson® is unmistakable. It has come to epitomise a lifestyle choice that represents freedom and independence

Founded in 1903, Harley-Davidson has always been about style and comfort, while also using technology to achieve the best possible performance from its ever-evolving machines. It also offers endless customisation opportunities to create a truly bespoke motorcycle. The Harley-Davidson® family encompasses everything from the classic Tourer to the more recent XR1200® – based on the legendary XR 750™, which was one of the most successful bikes in the history of motorcycle racing. What every model evokes is a passion for the open road.

harley-davidson.co.uk

Harman Kardon

Audio design innovation leader Harman Kardon combines simple, stylish looks with progressive technology, which has been making music sound its very best for over 50 years

It was a love of music that drove Dr Sidney Harman to create his first products in 1953. Since then, the Harman Kardon brand grew to become intrinsically linked with innovative audio technology for the home, the car and the computer. The groundbreaking SoundSticks, now regarded as a design classic, became the first branded computer speakers to win design awards. Harman Kardon was also one of the first companies to embrace HD technologies as well as recognise the need for iPod-compatible equipment. As music evolves, so too does Harman Kardon.

harman/kardon

harmankardon.com

ICA

London's ICA is one of the world's most innovative, multi-disciplinary arts centres and is home to the best of new artistic and cultural thinking from across the globe

The Institute of Contemporary Arts was established in 1947 by a collective of artists, poets, philosophers and writers to explore contemporary culture across the broadest range of art forms. Always at the forefront of cultural revolution, it has presented some of the most radical exhibitions, artists, films, music and thinking to have shaped our world. It continues today as a committed proponent of 'now', presenting a unique programme of visual arts, film, talks, music, and other special events in a new and experimental way.

ica.org.uk

James Brown London

Fashion and celebrity hairstylist James Brown joined forces with best friend Kate Moss in 2007, to bring a credibly cool haircare brand to the British high street, launched exclusively at Boots

James Brown London's promise of giving consumers access to the advice, trends and products previously only available to the fashion world and James' close-knit group of famous girlfriends has struck a chord. The brand has grown rapidly within its two years, with retail sales growth of over 100% in 2008, increased UK distribution through Boots and international outlets including cool retail Mecca, Colette in Paris. Summer 2009 saw the launch of a second haircare collection called Scandalous and the opening of James' first hair salon in London's West End.

jamesbrownlondon.com

Jelly Belly®

Since transforming the world of jelly beans in 1976, Jelly Belly® beans have been surprising the world's taste buds with small but perfectly formed bursts of flavour

It's the intense, really, really real taste, smaller size and brilliant colours of Jelly Belly that make it different. Developed for the sophisticated palate, natural ingredients such as fruit purées are used, when possible, to flavour the beans from the shell right to the centre. The Jelly Belly range consists of 50 official flavours and is sold in more than 50 countries worldwide. However, you can create new and individual flavours by combining beans according to their suggested 'recipes', or your own.

jellybelly-uk.com

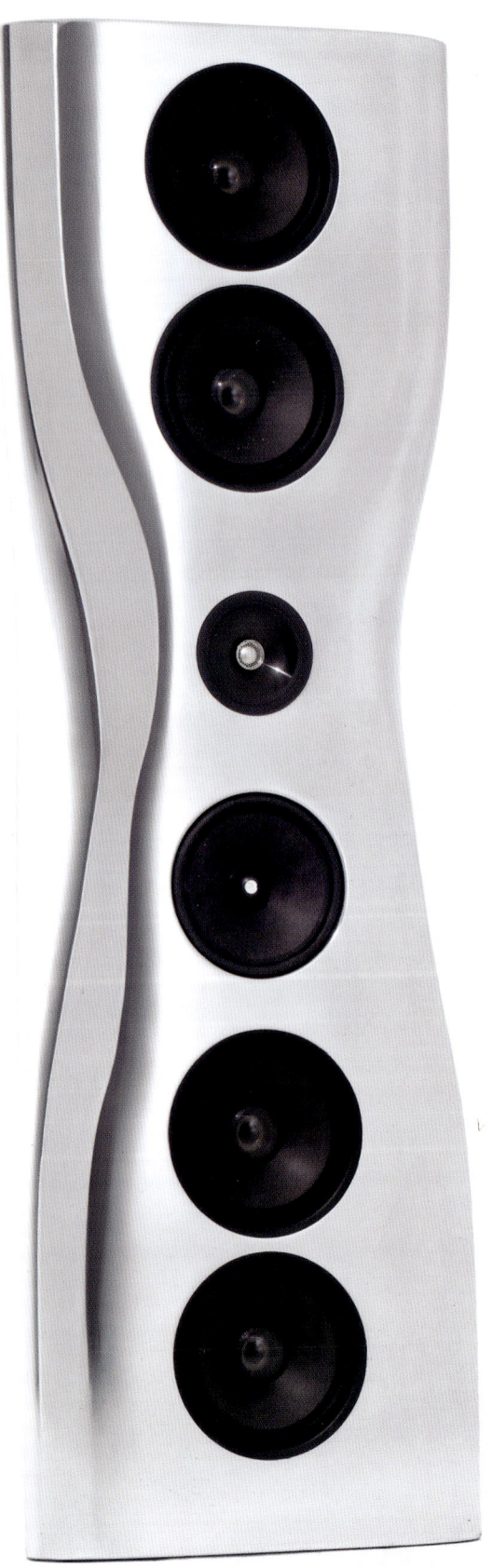

Muon

KEF

With a history of innovation stretching back nearly 50 years, British high-fidelity loudspeaker expert KEF has one of the best international reputations for audio excellence

Founded in 1961 by Raymond Cooke, KEF's reputation as the leader in loudspeaker engineering was soon set in stone. With such a pedigree, KEF has developed a flair for unusual and controversial engineering, design and use of materials, and has been the UK market leader in home-cinema speaker systems for the past five years. KEF's Muon loudspeakers, whose radical design is only matched by their incredible sound quality, confirm the brand's status as a pioneer in the field.

kef.com

The multi-award-winning KHT3005SE home-cinema system

Kéraskin Esthetics

Designed as a made-to-measure approach to skincare, Kéraskin Esthetics combines the most advanced active ingredients with professional expertise to maintain the skin's perfect cellular balance

For Kéraskin Esthetics, ideal skin is a perfect balance, a harmonious communication between the cells of the skin and their environment. Created by professionals, the brand offers a made-to-measure approach to skincare, which it calls the Cellular Re-Harmonisation Programme. The range combines the most advanced technologies and active ingredients from the L'Oréal laboratories, to offer a selection of bespoke facials and treatments and exclusive products that work to maintain cellular harmony at home.

keraskin-esthetics.com

Kérastase

The most advanced formulations, the most luxurious environments and the expertise of the Kérastase Specialist are the brand's ingredients to transform hair beauty into a skilful art form

Since its launch in 1964, Kérastase has been an innovator in the luxury haircare sector, creating advanced formulations that offer deep, intense hair transformation through pioneering technology from Recherche Avancée L'Oréal laboratories. In-salon treatments from the Kérastase Ritual Collection are complemented by a comprehensive, customised home-care range. Kérastase has become an iconic brand for millions, stocked in the finest salons and adored by influential hairdressers, celebrities and journalists worldwide.

kerastase.com

KÉRASTASE
PARIS

KETTLE® Chips

KETTLE® Chips likes to keep things simple by using quality potatoes that are hand cooked and seasoned using real ingredients and absolutely nothing artificial

Introduced to the UK in 1988, KETTLE® Chips is the number one hand-cooked crisp brand in the UK. The chips are made with top-quality potatoes, sunflower oil and authentic seasonings – hand cooked in small batches to give them a distinctive flavour, crunch and golden colour. The people at KETTLE® Chips have always believed that the simple approach to good food is best, so no artificial colours, flavourings, preservatives, or MSG are added during the cooking process.

kettlefoods.co.uk

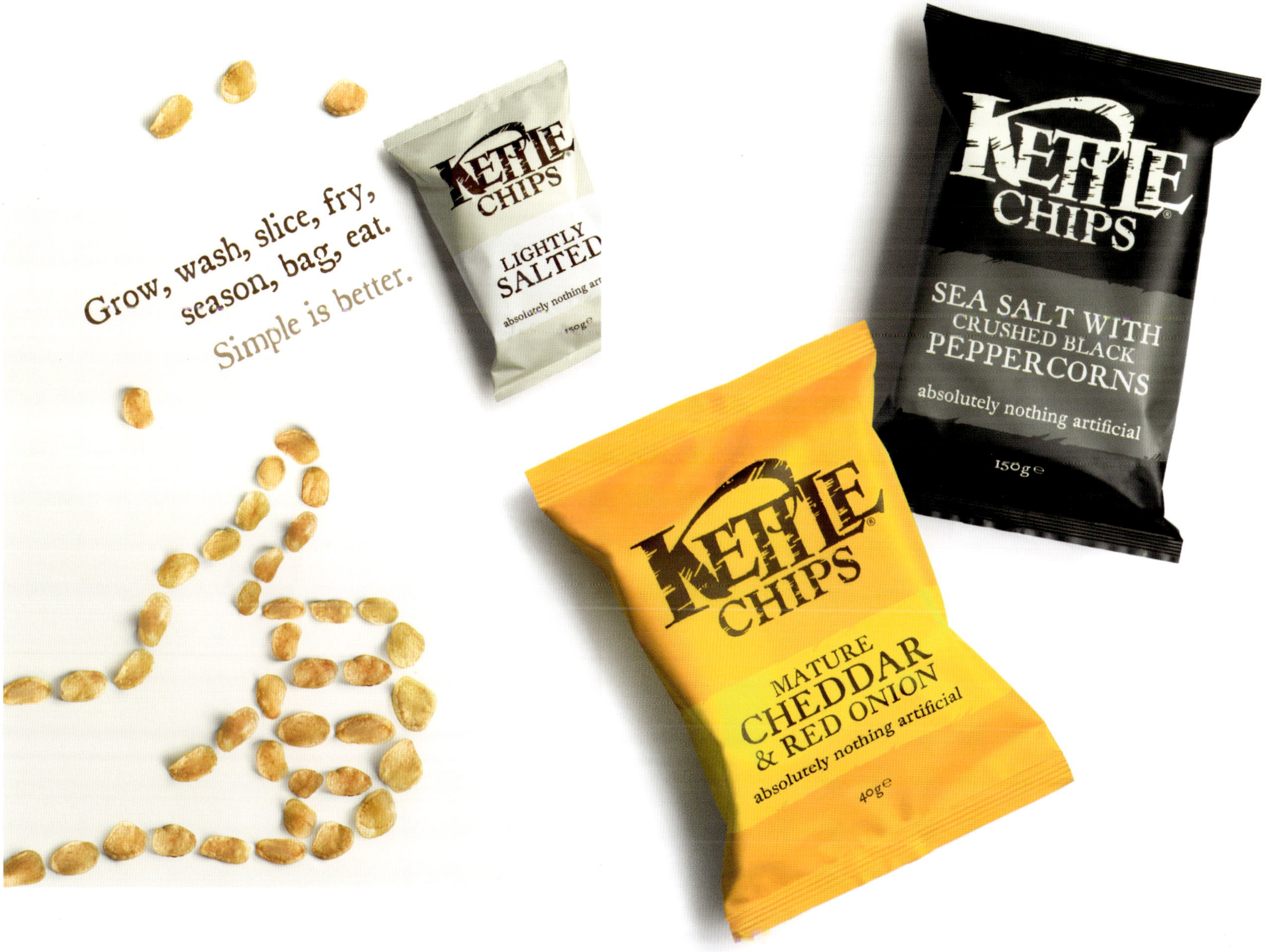

Grow, wash, slice, fry, season, bag, eat.
Simple is better.

LIGHTLY SALTED
absolutely nothing artificial
150g℮

SEA SALT WITH CRUSHED BLACK PEPPERCORNS
absolutely nothing artificial
150g℮

MATURE CHEDDAR & RED ONION
absolutely nothing artificial
40g℮

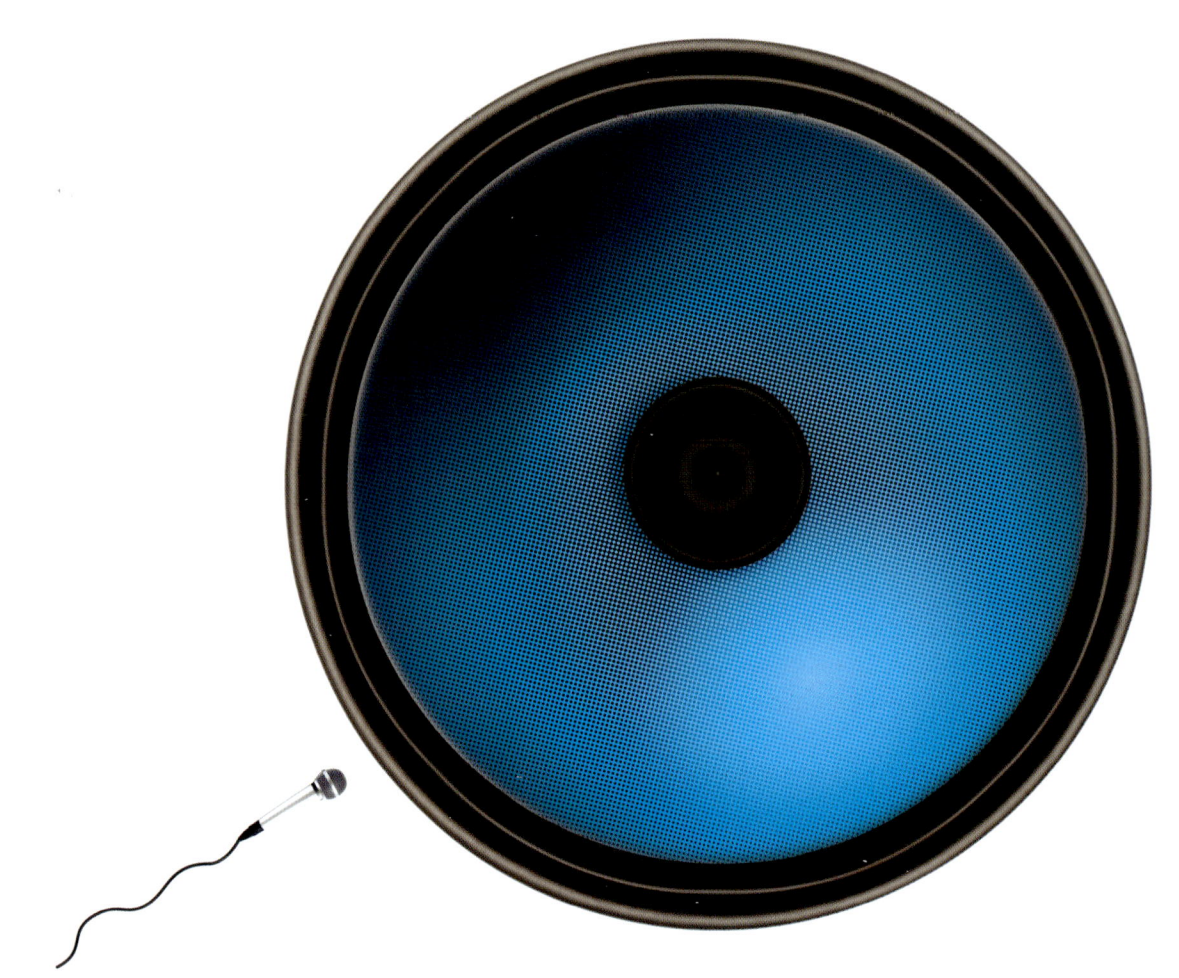

Music Is Life

Kiss

Connecting millions of consumers every week through radio and TV, Kiss consistently delivers the best in dance, hip hop and R&B

Kiss has one central belief: Music Is Life. This is the DNA that binds together its UK radio, TV and online audience. The Kiss mission is to Never Stand Still. It does this by constantly feeding its fans with the newest dance, hip hop and R&B, as well as reviews on the latest movies, gadgets and games. Shared music and lifestyle passions have driven audiences in 2009 to their highest level in its history.

totalkiss.com

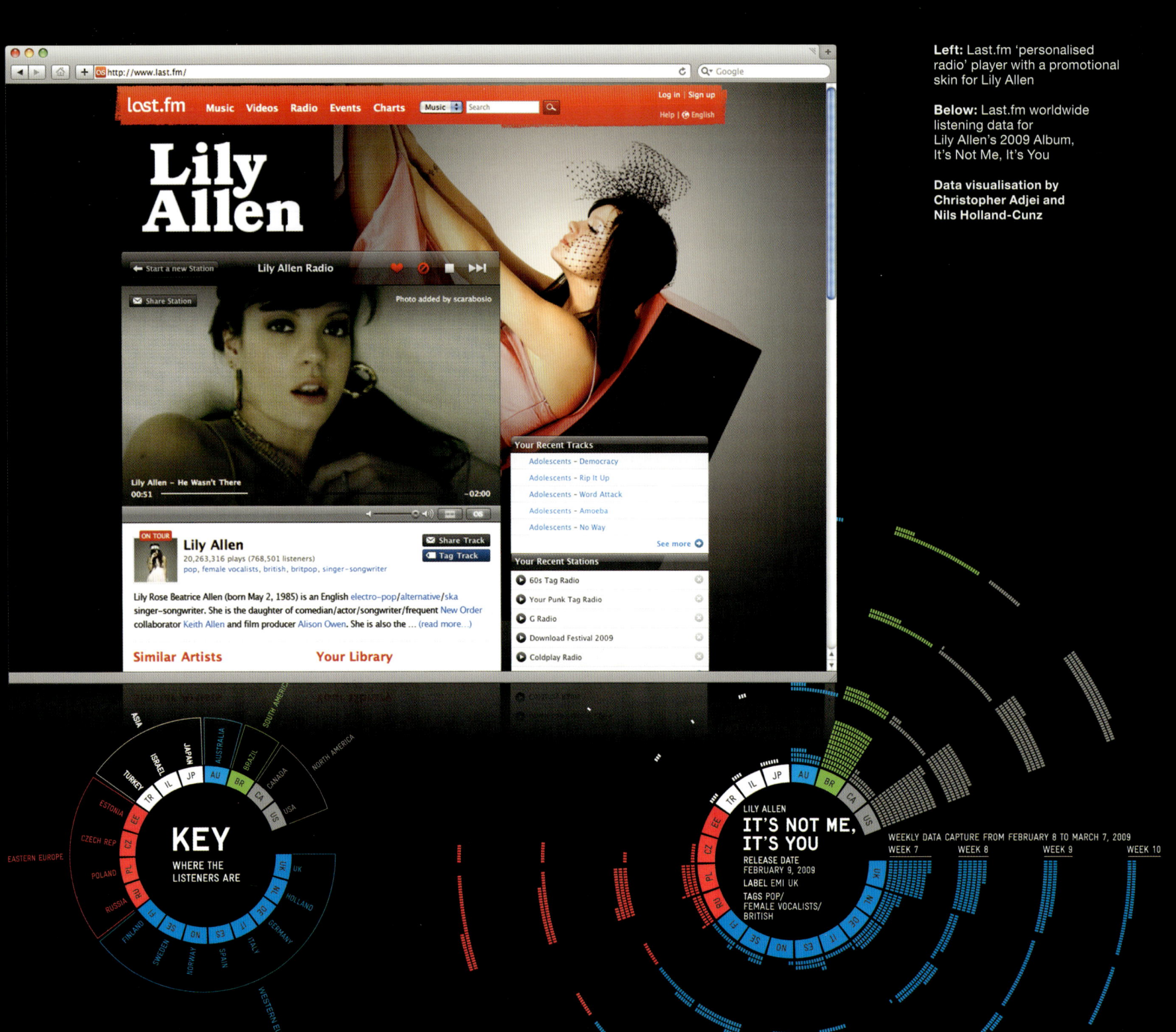

Left: Last.fm 'personalised radio' player with a promotional skin for Lily Allen

Below: Last.fm worldwide listening data for Lily Allen's 2009 Album, It's Not Me, It's You

Data visualisation by Christopher Adjei and Nils Holland-Cunz

Last.fm

Last.fm offers an innovative listening experience and comprehensive music library. As one of the web's best music discoveries, it has a community of 30 million passionate music fans

Last.fm is about discovering, listening to and sharing new music. The site uses its 'scrobbling' technology, active social network and expansive music library to create music recommendations tailored to each individual user. The site's six million-plus tracks can be streamed using Last.fm's multisensory 'personalised radio' player, which combines the audio and visual experience into one innovative listening experience.

last.fm

last.fm

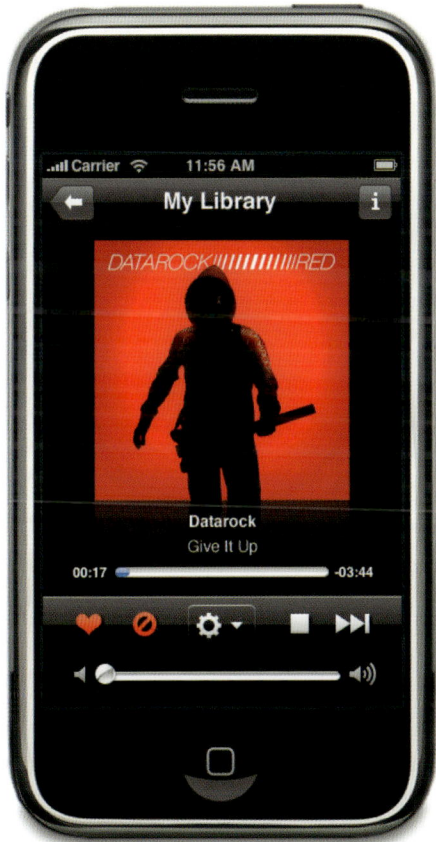

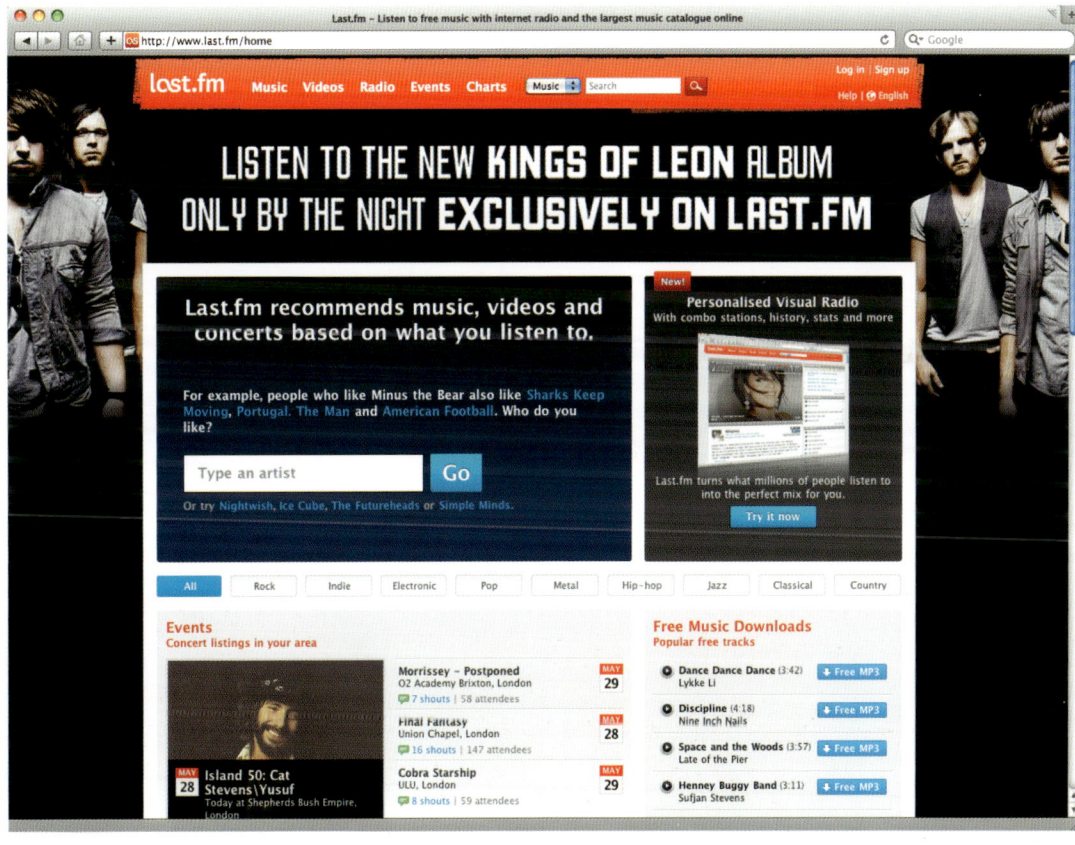

Leatherman®

The Leatherman® brand name is synonymous with quality and innovation and is the world leader in multi-tools

In 1975, Tim Leatherman found himself travelling through Europe on a tight budget in an unreliable car. His trusty scout knife just wasn't up to the challenges he faced during his 10-month journey. Tim wished he had a compact knife with full-sized pliers. When he returned to the USA, he put his engineering skills to work and after seven years, the original Leatherman® tool was perfected. There are now 11 tools in the Leatherman range to suit a multitude of tasks.

leatherman.co.uk

LEATHERMAN
Now you're ready.™

LG

LG Electronics offers a combination of stylish design and smart technology that enhances people's lives

LG Electronics has a history of bringing consumers products that are stylish in design, while encompassing the best in technology. This heritage, coupled with high-profile partnerships, such as Formula 1™, the LG Arena and the LG Big Air snowboarding event, has seen LG experience tremendous growth in its brand awareness. The company's slogan, 'Life's Good', is core to its evolution – where an awareness of the customer's changing needs continues to be at the heart of everything LG does.

lge.com/uk

Mr & Mrs Smith

Irreverent, stylish and original, the Mr & Mrs Smith brand represents a trusted source of information and recommendations for boutique-hotel lovers

There are some incredible places to stay – you just need the right help to find them. Meet Mr & Mrs Smith, the boutique travel experts. An acclaimed travel publisher and hotel booking service founded in London in 2003, Mr & Mrs Smith specialises in individual and boutique hotels – the world's coolest, sexiest and most intimate places to spend the night. The name is a wink to couples everywhere who fancy checking into a fabulous hotel under this classic naughty-weekend-away pseudonym.

mrandmrssmith.com

nails inc.

Ten years old this year, nails inc. is the ultimate in affordable pampering luxury with its pioneering 15-minute express manicures and high-quality, catwalk-inspired products

The launch pad for nails inc. was its trademark 15-minute manicure, which pioneered professional, high-quality nail treatments for women with little time to spare. Formulated with the latest professional technologies, the brand's fashion-forward range of colours also makes it a regular favourite on the London Fashion Week circuit. With three stand-alone stores in London and department-store concessions throughout the UK and Ireland, nails inc. also recently launched its exclusive Champagne Nail Bar concept in Harvey Nichols stores, as well as at Heathrow's Terminal 5.

nailsinc.com

nails inc.
LONDON

Olympus

A name that goes hand-in-hand with great photography, Olympus creates stylish cameras that make superb pictures achievable for everyone, from the beginner to the seasoned professional

With 90 years of optical expertise and a portfolio covering everything from research microscopes to fibre-optic products for keyhole surgery, Olympus is an imaging pioneer. The company's philosophy is to combine technical performance with ease of use and great design. Signature camera ranges like the Mju have become firm favourites with millions of photographers. The latest to join them is the remodelled Olympus PEN, which gives professional results with compact style and simplicity.

olympus.co.uk/pen

OLYMPUS

Legendary designer, Yoshihisa Maitani with an original PEN camera, from the range he developed

Orange

The best-known brand of the France Telecom Group, with over 180 million customers across 32 countries, Orange covers internet, television and mobile services

Orange provides mobile, broadband and entertainment services, guided by the global brand vision 'Together We Can Do More'. This is reflected in projects such as RockCorps, Orange's music-led volunteer programme, where music fans volunteer at special community-based charity projects in return for exclusive gig tickets. Orange is also a regular at festivals such as Glastonbury. Film is important to the brand, with Orange Wednesdays, the 2-for-1 cinema tickets deal, now in its fifth year. In addition, a new series of the much-loved Orange Gold Spot cinema ads has hit the screens.

orange.co.uk

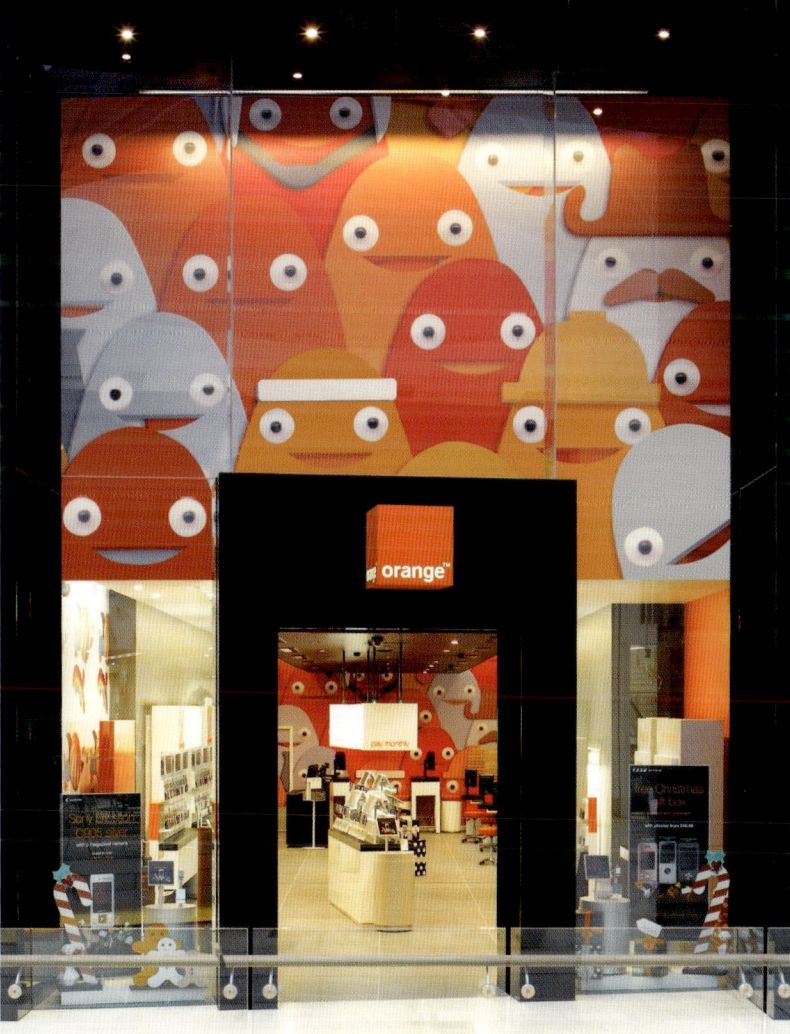

The new PS3 Slim

PlayStation®

Launched in Japan in 1994, PlayStation® is synonymous with gaming. Always breaking new technological boundaries, its aim is to offer the unexpected and keep gamers surprised

Gaming on the PlayStation®, now in its third incarnation, has evolved from using a disc with one beginning, middle and end, to a high-definition experience where the game is just the start. Now music, movies, internet and communications are possible, expanding the PlayStation® experience way beyond the traditional concept of gaming. PSP™ (PlayStation Portable), a hand-held games console, makes gaming anywhere a reality, and the PS3 Slim, a new lighter, more streamlined version of the PlayStation 3, is the jewel in the console-maker's crown.

uk.playstation.com

PLAYSTATION 3

Poggenpohl

Synonymous with innovative design, Poggenpohl is the world's best-known luxury kitchen brand. Founded in 1892, Poggenpohl continues to challenge convention and inspire new trends

Spearheading innovation in kitchen design, Poggenpohl is renowned for its uncompromising build-quality and engineering excellence. Founder Friedemir Poggenpohl's mission to 'improve the kitchen' is still central to the brand's design ethos. Exceptional form and function create designs that transform domestic spaces and remain contemporary icons for decades. Nowhere is this more evident than in Poggenpohl's latest innovation, the Dining Desk, a concept that is perfectly in tune with the evolving role of the kitchen in the modern home.

poggenpohl.com

Pret A Manger

Since 1986, Pret has been creating handmade, natural food, avoiding the additives and preservatives commonly found in so much of the fast food on the market today

Key to Pret's success is its passion for producing freshly prepared, good, natural food served by proud, professional people. Nearly all Pret shops have their own kitchens and daily deliveries of ingredients ensure that food is always fresh, eliminating the need for sell-by dates. Food that is unsold at the end of the day is offered to charities working with the homeless. Pret now has 225 shops in the UK, New York, Washington DC and Hong Kong.

pret.com

Proud Galleries

One of the world's foremost rock 'n' roll photography galleries and live music venues, Proud Galleries comprises three exhibition spaces over its two Central London sites

Innovative, informal and increasingly infamous, Proud began in 1998 as a trailblazing gallery exhibiting some of the world's best rock 'n' roll photography, and has since gone on to build an enviable reputation as one of the most influential venues on the capital's live music and bar scene. The Proud Horse Hospital venue offers music-lovers – from musicians to fashionistas, students to celebs – the chance to experience memorable and intimate live gigs, surrounded by striking music imagery.

proud.co.uk

Ray-Ban

Built on a reputation for quality, innovation and style, Ray-Ban, the world's best-selling eyewear brand, is the choice of the greats of rock 'n' roll and film

In 1929, revolutionary lightweight Aviator sunglasses were created for American pilots, marking an auspicious beginning for Ray-Ban. The iconic Wayfarer was launched in 1952 and made famous by Audrey Hepburn in Breakfast at Tiffany's. Wayfarers have since graced the faces of generations of heart-throbs and rock gods. Now the relaunched, 50s-inspired Clubmaster, reinterpreted in bold colours, has become another must-have accessory. Meanwhile, the Ray-Ban Tech collection breaks new ground, using highly advanced Carbon Fibre and P3 lens technology.

ray-ban.com

Roberts Radio

Founded in 1932, Roberts Radio is the UK brand leader in the portable radio market and is sold everywhere around the world from Japan to the USA

With a reputation built on producing high-quality, reliable radios, Roberts continues to lead the way with a range of over 100 different DAB, analogue, world radios, radio cassettes and internet radios. Roberts remains at the forefront of product development and innovation and introduced PausePlus, CD and SD bookmark, radios with Electronic Programme Guides, as well as WiFi to the market. Roberts is also responsible for industry firsts, including a DAB/FM radio for the iPod and the first truly portable DAB/WiFi radio.

ROBERTS

robertsradio.co.uk

Rough Trade Shops

Where commercial transactions have the air of gifts, Rough Trade stores have the rare ability to excite. If music's your religion, Rough Trade's your church

Founded in 1976, Rough Trade shops have emerged from the punk movement to become today's most credible music retail brand, with their independent roots remaining proudly intact. Once partnered with the Rough Trade record label, they have been separately run and owned since the early 80s. Today, with Rough Trade East and West stores, a new digital store and a reputation for peerless recommendation authority, their future looks brighter than ever.

roughtrade.com

ROUGH TRADE

Roundhouse

The Roundhouse gives young people a chance to realise their creativity and offers audiences of all ages new and extraordinary experiences in live music, theatre, dance, circus and new media

From modest Victorian beginnings as a steam engine repair shed to legendary cultural venue, the Roundhouse has an enviable heritage. The Grade II listed building is now home to a bold and exciting programme of international performing arts and a state-of-the-art creative centre exclusively for 11- to 25-year-olds. Young people are at the heart of everything the Roundhouse does: they're on its board and help plan and perform at events. The venue is also available for exclusive hire for events catering for between 20 and 1,800 people.

roundhouse.org.uk

Russian Standard Vodka

The global leader in the authentic Russian premium vodka market still conforms to the original formula established in 1894 by famed scientist Dmitri Mendeleev

The water used to produce Russian Standard Vodka originates from Lake Ladoga in the glacial north of Russia, providing ideal softness for distillation, while the wheat that creates the subtle, bread-like taste is harvested from the southern steppes. Founded in 1998, Russian Standard Original can now be found in 65 countries across the world. Russian Standard Platinum and luxury brand Imperia have also been added to the portfolio.

russianstandardvodka.com

Sanderson

A lavish 'urban spa' in the heart of London, Sanderson blends wit, magic and surprise in an elegant balancing act of extravagance and simplicity

Just because you stay in a hotel doesn't mean you have to be confined to reality. A daring Cocteau-like dreamworld and personal revitalisation programme wrapped into one, Sanderson is a surreal fantasy, where you can expect the unexpected. The landmark 50s building has been transformed by Philippe Starck and epitomises a new luxury that is smart, pared down and tempered with a healthy dose of wit and irony.

SANDERSON

sandersonlondon.com

End call

02:03

Turn off video

Skype

The telephone was fine for saying a simple 'Hello', but for really reaching out to each other, something more powerful was needed. That something was Skype

In 2003, Skype's aim was to take 'Hello' and lift it to 'It's so good to see you!'. It had a fresh idea – and its simple mission was to give everyone a better way to talk to each other, for as long as they liked, wherever they were in the world. Six years on, Skype is on computers, cordless devices and mobiles – so even people on the move can stay in touch without cost, or distance, standing in their way.

skype.com

St Martins Lane

With its daring disregard for convention, uncompromising attention to detail and flawless personal service, St Martins Lane challenges the notion of what makes an urban hotel

A luminous jewel set in the West End of London, St Martins Lane is a dramatic and daring reinvention of the urban resort. Smart, witty and sophisticated, Philippe Starck's design is a brilliant collision of influences – from the modern to the baroque – that suffuses the hotel with energy, vitality and magic. At Asia de Cuba, restaurateur Jeffrey Chodorow has created a dynamic menu that blends Latin and Asian cuisine, with stunning results.

ST MARTINS LANE

stmartinslane.com

St. Tropez

Renowned for its skin finishing expertise, the mission of St. Tropez is to develop a beauty regime that creates flawless, stylishly tanned and radiant skin

Market leaders in self tanning, innovation is key to this award-winning brand. Among St. Tropez's new product developments is Aromaguard™, a technology that eliminates self-tan odour by a minimum of 70%. Always on-trend, St. Tropez led the way at London Fashion Week's SS 2010 shows, with models showcasing a variety of tanning products and looks. Due to the self-esteem boosting nature of its products, the company works closely with the Prince's Trust and, as a safe-sun educator, has spearheaded a campaign for stricter regulations on sunbeds in the UK.

st-tropez.com

ST.TROPEZ

Stella Artois

Only those who appreciate the true worth of the world's most popular Belgian beer deserve to hear those hallowed words, 'une Stella Artois pour Monsieur'

With heritage dating back to 1366, Stella Artois has a space reserved in the hand and heart of many a beer lover. Crafted using only four ingredients and served in the iconic chalice glass, the brand is famed for its cinematic tales about the sacrifices beer connoisseurs will make for it. The launch of Stella Artois 4% sees the brand saunter into the 1960s to become the toast of the Riviera, introducing smooth characters and their equally smooth escapades.

smoothoriginals.com

Interview

Emma
WATSON
Unveiled!

MAY | $4.99

015117

0 092816 8

05>

Storm

Launching the careers of some of the defining individuals of our time, Storm is a major player in a fashion industry that has globalised beyond recognition over the past 22 years

Storm Model Management has over 20 years' experience discovering and developing the careers of some of fashion's most famous faces. Offering expert guidance and fostering longevity in careers based on talent and integrity, Storm has cultivated a list of clients that includes Kate Moss, Lily Cole, Cindy Crawford, Eva Herzigova, Jourdan Dunn and Alek Wek. Storm expanded this philosophy by establishing a Special Bookings Division that provides commercial opportunities for talented individuals including Emma Watson, Lily Allen and Michael Bublé.

stormmodels.com

storm

Tanqueray gin

Charles Tanqueray began distilling in 1830 and his legacy of excellence continues with Tanqueray® gin – a spirit with an elegance and sophistication that warrant its premium status

He was expected to become a clergyman, but Charles Tanqueray broke with tradition to follow his passion and, in 1830, began distilling gin. His curiosity and refusal to accept the predictable, combined with years of experimentation, led to the creation of this vibrant, award-winning, 'un-simple' gin. Tanqueray® is the premium gin of choice for the world's top bartenders, who regard it as a spirit with an unmatched depth of flavour.

tanqueray.com

The Cinnamon Club

The Cinnamon Club's mission is to set a new benchmark for excellence in London's restaurant scene, by combining the finest ingredients, innovative cooking and grand surroundings

Celebrating innovation, creativity, spirit and life, the focus of the cuisine at The Cinnamon Club is to demonstrate how a new chapter in gourmet excellence can be shaped by evolving and adapting. Housed in The Old Westminster Library, a stone's throw from Westminster Abbey, The Cinnamon Club's unique surroundings complement its distinctive style of new Indian cuisine. It believes that combining this with charming and attentive service creates one of the finest restaurants in the world.

cinnamonclub.com

THE CINNAMON CLUB

THE CINNAMON CLUB

The Perfect Venue for Your Special Event.

Enjoy exquisite modern Indian cuisine in the unique setting of the Grade II Listed former Westminster Library.

The award winning Cinnamon Club offers a wide range of private rooms ideal for almost any event from canapé receptions and gastronomic dinners to birthday parties and weddings.

The Private Dining Room and Mezzanine both reflect the history of the building whilst in contrast the subterranean Cinnamon Club Bar has a very contemporary feel. The Main Dining Room is also available for exclusive hire.

For further information or to arrange a visit, contact our dedicated events team at: events@cinnamonclub.com or on +44 (0)20 7222 2555
The Old Westminster Library
30-32 Great Smith Street London SW1P 3BU

WEDDINGS

COCKTAIL PARTIES

CORPORATE EVENTS

Product Launches

BREAKFAST MEETINGS

CELEBRATIONS

Wine Tasting

Special Occasions

PRIVATE DINING

The Glenlivet

The definitive single malt whisky that put Speyside, Scotland's best-known whisky-producing region on the map, is The Glenlivet, 'The single malt that started it all'

Today George Smith's original single malt has evolved into a definitive range of individual quality whiskies; while each retains its own distinctive character and style, all bear the unmistakable hallmark of The Glenlivet. The rich choice of the range provides an opportunity to select the ideal malt for any occasion. The Glenlivet has consistently won awards for its finesse, complexity and superb balance. 'The single malt that started it all' is still leading the way.

theglenlivet.com

The Zetter

With its strong identity and affordable price tag, The Zetter changed people's preconceptions of boutique hotels for good, making it the original small hotel with a big personality

The Zetter's opening in 2004 heralded a new era for London's now über trendy Clerkenwell. Reinventing the boutique-hotel concept, The Zetter shunned stark minimalism and embraced bold architectural design, retro detailing and statement pieces. The brainchild of restaurateurs Mark Sainsbury and Michael Benyan, The Zetter's restaurant and bar have become neighbourhood as well as international favourites, and with a new Clerkenwell townhouse due to open next year, all eyes will be on The Zetter.

thezetter.com

Virgin Atlantic

Known for its innovation and service quality, Virgin Atlantic is one of the world's leading long-haul airlines. Its mission is to be an everyday pioneer for the modern traveller

Virgin Atlantic was launched in June 1984 with just one Boeing 747 flying between London Gatwick and Newark International, New York. Now, 25 years later, its London-based fleet of 38 aircraft travels to 30 destinations worldwide. Virgin Atlantic flies the same planes from the same airports as its bigger rivals, but continually aims to offer a superior service. From its vibrant cabin crew and award-winning Clubhouses, to its extensive on-board entertainment, Virgin Atlantic strives to prove consistently that flying can be a fantastic experience.

virginatlantic.com

Wahaca

Vibrant, imaginative and affordable, Wahaca brings the spirit of Mexican market eating to the UK, with an approach that's as fresh as the irresistible street food on its menu

Hibiscus margaritas served in recycled glass; soft corn tacos rolled around fresh seafood; street art on the walls. Enter Wahaca and you would be forgiven for thinking that you had stepped into a Mexican street market. Founded by Mark Selby and Masterchef 2005 winner Thomasina Miers, with branding from London-based BuroCreative, Wahaca introduces real Mexican street food to the UK with a menu as colourful as its style. Queues outside and a coveted Observer Food Monthly Award testify to its winning formula.

wahaca.co.uk

wahaca
mexican
market
eating

Yauatcha

The all-day dim sum tea house that is Yauatcha was launched in 2004 by Alan Yau. Its aim is to offer high-quality casual dining

Alan Yau's trademark approach marries high-quality cuisine with cutting-edge interior design. This formula gained immediate critical acclaim, with Yauatcha being heralded at launch as Newcomer of the Year by the Harper's and Moët Restaurant Awards. The restaurant went on to secure a Michelin Star within a year of opening. The menu at Yauatcha is primarily dim sum, with about 10 dishes forming a generic definition of this way of eating, but with a distinctive, modernised twist.

YAUATCHA 丘記茶苑

yauatcha.com

From its early uploads filmed on low-fi camcorders, YouTube has evolved to encompass full-length HD feature films (Luc Besson's 'Home', bottom left), experiments with 3D visuals (top left) and premium web series such as The Station (bottom right). The YouTube Symphony Orchestra at Carnegie Hall (top right) was a groundbreaking piece of online collaboration through video, and the platform continues to showcase compelling content from premium creators, partners and users (see facing page).

YouTube

Users, content creators and advertisers use YouTube to connect, inform and inspire others across the globe through sharing online video

On YouTube people view themselves not as passive recipients of broadcast content, but active participants in the creative process. Aspiring musicians shoot to recognition and record deals via home videos broadcast globally. Politicians use YouTube to connect with voters and raise awareness of issues. Educational groups create e-learning videos for parents. In addition, established media companies and advertisers use this platform to market and interact with people, harnessing their ingenuity and enthusiasm in ways that were unimaginable 10 years ago.

youtube.com

Expert Council
2009/10

Expert Council 2009/10

At the core of the decision-making process of CoolBrands® 2009/10 are 33 council members. These are the style leaders, creative thinkers and media movers and shakers of our generation who have genuine insight into what constitutes 'cool'.

Walé Adeyemi

Fashion Designer

Stylist to international A-list stars, Walé has become one of the UK's most recognised and successful fashion designers since he emerged on the scene in 1998.

He has spoken at Oxford University, and is a proud Prince's Trust Ambassador. Walé was awarded an MBE for his services to fashion in 2008.

Simon Armstrong

Head of Retail
Design Museum

Simon Armstrong is head of retail at the Design Museum in London, where he sources, commissions and sells design products, books and artwork from all over the world.

Simon is resident DJ for the Friends And Family London club night at Cargo, and has performed around the UK and Europe, as well as at music festivals including The Big Chill and V Festival. He also writes the design blog Keep Left.

Niku Banaie

Managing Director
Isobar Global

Niku joined Isobar, one of the world's leading full-service digital networks, in June 2008. Prior to this he was the youngest partner at Naked Communications, London, where he created award-winning work for Honda, Orange, E4 and Nike among others.

Niku's career had a strong start when he graduated from Central Saint Martins College of Art & Design with Distinction.

Other projects include brothersister, a furniture label that can be found in the V&A.

'A cool brand has the ability to harness creativity with integrity.'

Simon Armstrong
Head of Retail, Design Museum

'Cool is a brand that stays true to its values and principles, abiding by them no matter how tough it becomes. A brand generating positive word of mouth and social currency, by challenging the norm in an effortlessly understated way.
    I'm not certain we all agree, or understand, what makes a brand cool. However, I know it's something we covet, we need to be seen with, and can't live without.'

Lee Farrant
Partner, RPM Group

Damian Barr

Journalist, Writer, Playwright & Presenter

Damian Barr tells stories. Some of them are true, some just might be. He writes and blogs regularly for The Times, and was described as 'the new ringmaster for the Jerry Springer generation' by Julie Burchill for his book about the 'quarterlife' crisis.

His plays have been heard on BBC Radio 4 and Damian can often be found in hotels as a reader in residence – a literary call boy to be summoned to read in your room. He also hosts the hugely successful Literary Salons at Shoreditch and Soho Houses.

Ed Bartlam

**Co-Founder & Director
Underbelly Ltd**

Ed founded Underbelly at the Edinburgh Festival in 2000, at the age of 19. Growing rapidly from a small scale Fringe venue, it is now the third-largest venue in Edinburgh. Through Underbelly, Ed manages comedians, books comedy for music festivals and tours the 'upside-down cow' Udderbelly tent to other cities and festivals.

In 2006, Ed won the award for Outstanding Off Stage Contribution at the Chortle Live Comedy Awards.

Edith Bowman

Radio & TV Broadcaster

Edith got her break at MTV on Daily Edition and Hitlist UK. In 2003 she joined Radio 1 and has presented the Edith Bowman Show on weekday afternoons since 2006.

Television presenting roles have included RI:SE (C4), Top Of The Pops (BBC1), Rough Guide To The World (BBC2), New Kings Of Rock 'n' Roll, and 4 Music Specials (C4).

Edith also hosts the BBC's television coverage of Glastonbury, the Reading and Leeds festivals, T in the Park and BBC Radio 1's Big Weekend.

'It's about being honest, treating the environment kindly, simple and useful design, constantly innovating – fundamentally saying and doing something different from the pack.'

Niku Banaie
Managing Director, Isobar Global

'Cool is honest and honestly not trying.'

Damian Barr
Journalist, Writer, Playwright & Presenter

Kevin Braddock

**Contributing Editor
GQ**

Kevin is a journalist who has written about social trends, health & fitness, business, technology, youth culture, music and travel in all the UK's leading magazines and newspapers. He is contributing editor for GQ and was formerly features editor at The Face.

Kevin graduated with a First Class degree in European Languages from Goldsmiths College, and was nominated as PPA Writer of the Year in 2007.

Patrick Burgoyne

**Editor
Creative Review**

Patrick worked in marketing for The Body Shop and the University of Westminster before joining Creative Review as staff writer, and becoming editor in 1999.

He is the author of several books on design and visual culture, including Bored: Surf/Skate/Snow Graphics with designer Jeremy Leslie Patrick has also written for publications including The Independent, Scotland on Sunday, Graphis, La Repubblica and The Big Issue.

Neil Byrne

**Board Director
Camron**

Neil heads up the architecture division at Camron, the UK's leading design and architecture PR company. He has worked on many landmark architectural projects around the world, from China to the Middle East and America to Europe, giving him a global perspective on brands and a firm understanding of what makes a brand cool.

Neil currently leads the PR team for The Shard, Renzo Piano's new London Bridge skyscraper.

'I think something that makes a bit of a statement and stands out from the rest makes a cool brand. Individuality is important; so is something or someone who is starting a trend while still providing a great service. The scoring system was actually quite hard, but I had to be ruthless.'

Edith Bowman
Radio & TV Broadcaster

Kate Creasey

Editor
Cosmopolitan.co.uk

Kate is an award-winning online journalist and has been the editor of Cosmopolitan.co.uk since November 2007. Prior to a stint as a beauty editor, indulging a guilty obsession with make-up, creams and potions, Kate's career began in fashion, beauty and health PR.

With more than nine years' experience as an online editor, Kate is an authority on web trends and online publishing.

Sarah J Edwards

Director
BLAG UK Ltd

As co-founder, co-publisher, co-editor and photographic director of BLAG, Sarah's background is rooted in photography, music and publishing. Recently, she's worked with Franz Ferdinand, Rupert Grint, N*E*R*D, Adrien Brody, Queens of the Stone Age and MGMT for exclusive BLAG content.

She has an array of experience in publicity, having represented world-famous acts as well as interviewing and photographing many established and up-and-coming talents in music, film, fashion and art for national and international publications.

Lee Farrant

Partner
RPM Group

Lee is a photographer foremost and a businessman second. Since 1996, he has looked after creative services at the agency RPM London. These encompass design, creative, digital and, of course, photography.

He is an avid sportsman and cannily manages to combine this passion with the brands that he works for and the business that he loves. Lee strongly believes sport should be accessible to all, and is involved in a number of projects about encouraging participation at all levels.

'To me, cool is about standing out from the crowd. A person or brand who dares to be different.'

Kate Creasey
Editor, Cosmopolitan.co.uk

'As Edna Woolman Chase said: "Fashion can be bought. Style one must possess". Successful brands have to inhabit both areas from the outset, stay ahead of things in the future and all this with an added dash of iconography, and more than a hint of a successful business model, too. More than anything, a cool brand must be relevant and have enduring appeal.'

Sadie Frost
Actress & Fashion Designer

Sadie Frost

Actress & Fashion Designer

Sadie first trod the boards at Manchester's Royal Exchange Theatre under the direction of Nicholas Hytner. She appeared in Francis Ford Coppola's cult film, Dracula, and has had more than 20 other film and TV roles. In 2009, Sadie completed a successful West End run of the one-woman play Touched For The Very First Time.

Her fashion label FrostFrench was formed in 1999 with her best friend and designer Jemima French. They won Elle magazine's Designers of the Year Award 2004.

Sandra Halliday

Global Managing Editor, Real-Time Reporting & Analysis, WGSN

Sandra runs the news, business, celebrity and future analysis side of global intelligence firm WGSN, having worked there for nine years.

An experienced journalist, over the past 25 years she has morphed from fashion editor into fashion and beauty news and business writer. Sandra has also been a consultant for special projects within the cosmetics sector, as well as a frequent fashion industry commentator for the media.

Newby Hands

Associate Editor & Director of Health & Beauty, Harper's Bazaar

Newby was style & beauty editor at the Daily Mail before moving to Harper's Bazaar 13 years ago. In 2008, she was named Beauty Journalist of the Year at the P&G Beauty Awards, receiving an Achiever Award from CEW (UK) in the same year.

Newby's early career began with a buying course at Harrods. After this she worked in the music business before moving into fashion and journalism on the London Evening Standard.

'It's amazing how easy the scoring was – the brands that stood out as cool were just very obvious. They seem to have something in their DNA; an almost effortless ability to make us want and admire them.

Some other brands seem to try so hard to be cool but miss the point that great design, understanding your customer, a commitment to excellence and other such qualities are what should come first – coolness should follow in their wake.'

Sandra Halliday
Global Managing Editor, Real-Time Reporting & Analysis, WGSN

Andrew Harrison

**Associate Editor, The Word,
& Editor-in-Chief, Mixmag**

Andrew has worked with the new model independent publishers Development Hell Ltd since 2002. Here he co-launched The Word and was responsible for acquiring and revamping Mixmag.

Andrew was the first British writer to identify the transformative nature of the iPod, in Honey, I Shrunk The Record Collection (The Word, 2003). He has also written about music and popular culture for Rolling Stone, GQ, Arena, The Face, the Guardian, The Observer and Marie Claire.

Jack Horner

**Co-Founder & Creative Director,
FRUKT**

Jack has a background spanning music and communications including production, performance, education, artist management, major label international marketing and digital communications.

He is the founder of the only truly music-focussed strategy and communications agency, FRUKT. Clients include Coca-Cola, Arcadia Group, O2 and Sony Music. Jack also produces the future music business report, FRUKT Music Intelligence, as well as the music and branding blog, brandsbandsfans.com.

Lucy Johnston

**Brand Innovation Consultant
& Founder, The Neon Birdcage**

Lucy is former executive editor of the Global Innovation Report. She left this role and founded The Neon Birdcage, a curated insights and events platform for creative business. She is working with international companies and organisations including Mother London, American Express, Luxury Marketing Council, British Council and London 2012, alongside various cultural projects.

Lucy travels widely to deliver consultancy, host events and speak at conferences, and is working on a book promoting British creative talent. She is a fellow of the RSA and a selected member of the Courvoisier The Future 500 network.

'While criteria such as uniqueness, desirability and premium-ness are all sound considerations, a truly cool brand incorporates all these aspirational drivers, but still seems distinct from its peers.
  The combination of all those factors, along with an unquantifiable resonance with a particular moment in modern culture, results in a brand that transcends the pack.'

Jack Horner
Co-Founder & Creative Director, FRUKT

Dolly Jones

**Editor
VOGUE.COM**

During the journalism course that she undertook at the University of the Arts London, Dolly was told to interview someone at the top of their game. Alexandra Shulman kindly obliged. This eventually led to Dolly becoming a writer at Vogue.com in 2000.

She rose to become website editor in 2005 and leads this trusted authority on fashion, which incorporates a daily news service and coverage of every catwalk show in the world.

Katrina Larkin

**Co-Founder
The Big Chill**

Katrina formed The Big Chill in 1994 with Pete Lawrence, launching The Big Chill Festival the following year. She has also staged events in Goa, Cairo and Greece through The Big Chill, and established its record label.

In partnership with The Cantaloupe Group, The Big Chill Bar off London's Brick Lane was opened in 2005, followed in 2007 by The Big Chill House in King's Cross, with The Big Chill Bristol launching in October 2009.

Also in 2009, Katrina was creatively involved with Film4 and WarpX on a zombie film, I Spit On Your Rave, and published The Big Chill Guide to Summer Living, with Guardian Books.

Ben de Lisi

Fashion Designer

Ben studied sculpture at the Pratt Institute in Brooklyn before moving to London in 1982 and producing his first capsule collection. He has shown at London Fashion Week since 1995, and acted as a mentor on the TV show Project Catwalk.

Ben designs a diffusion line in conjunction with Debenhams, BDL by Ben de Lisi, and is building up his collections within the Debenhams umbrella with evening wear, daywear, childrenswear, accessories and homewear. Ben is also working on interior design projects and launching Ben de Lisi bathroom and kitchen showrooms around the country.

'A brand that I would define as cool makes me want it… makes me use it… makes me aspire to it… and becomes a bit of a status symbol. It has to be totally aspirational and at the top of its game.'

Ben de Lisi
Fashion Designer

'It's not about products that are hot, it's more about something that isn't just style over substance.'

Trevor Nelson
DJ

Kay McMahon

Digital Director
Wallpaper*

Kay launched handbag.com in 1999 and stayed on for eight years, during which time it was the UK's most popular women's website.

She left to join global design authority Wallpaper* magazine in April 2007, responsible for all things digital – including traffic growth, syndication, affiliations and new initiatives.

With more than 12 years' experience online, Kay's previous jobs have included radio production and management, advertising and technical writing. In addition, Kay has also DJ-ed intermittently for the past 20 years.

James Murphy

Founding Partner
adam & eve

In January 2008, James founded the much talked about start-up, adam & eve. The agency is currently number one in the UK new business league, having won accounts including John Lewis, Williams F1, The Telegraph Media Group, Westfield London, Lloyds London 2012 sponsorship, Bell's whisky and EMI Music.

Trevor Nelson

DJ

Trevor began his broadcasting career at the then pirate station Kiss FM, before going on to work in A&R for artists such as D'Angelo and signing Lynden David Hall.

He hosts the official start to the weekend on Radio 1, a soul and R&B show on Radio 2, the 1 Xtra weekly breakfast show, and also presents MTV's The Lick.

Trevor has been awarded an MBE for services to charity. He regularly DJs across Europe and has released five compilation albums.

'The challenge of judging is marrying that instant emotional response to a brand with a more thoughtful review of its current image and positioning.'

Jess Search
Chief Executive, Channel 4 BRITDOC Foundation

'I guess something that is cool must be effortless. And it is obviously much easier to become un-cool. Cool is subjective. I saw this first-hand as new boy on the judging panel, with many hours of debate on what makes a brand cool. As a judge on many panels, this was one of the most stringent and strict experiences I've come across – very impressive.'

Steve Parkinson
Managing Director, London Radio, Bauer Media

Steve Parkinson

**Managing Director, London Radio
Bauer Media**

Steve Parkinson has been at the helm of Kiss FM for three years, in that time overseeing a new generation of young talent and music DJs, and a newly evolved image. Radio is certainly not dead to younger consumers, as the network's biggest ever audience proves.

Steve understands 'youth', having been the first managing director of the Galaxy network, launching it across the UK in the 1990s.

Lauretta Roberts

**Digital Development Director
WGSN**

Lauretta took on her current role at Emap's global trend and style forecasting business, WGSN, in July 2009. Prior to this she edited fashion business bible Drapers, relaunching the magazine and introducing its first content-driven website with daily news service.

Lauretta has 12 years' experience in business writing and editing which spans sectors from print media and publishing to live events, design and fashion. She also acts as a judge for several fashion industry awards and often appears in the media as an industry commentator.

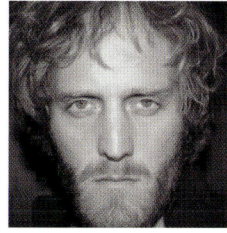

Nicolas Roope

**Founding Partner
Poke London**

Nicolas is an impassioned digital media visionary with a career spanning 14 years. He co-founded and is creative director at Poke. He also founded the cult electronics brand Hulger (www.hulger.com), and has three products in MoMA's permanent design collection in New York.

Nicolas is a member of the Academy of Digital Arts and Sciences and UK Webby Ambassador.

'It's completely instinctive. I went with my first reaction – it's usually the most accurate. That's what people do when they buy something in a shop – either they connect immediately or they don't. People don't spend too much time analysing whether or not something is cool.'

Lauretta Roberts
Digital Development Director, WGSN

Tom Savigar

**Partner
The Future Laboratory**

Tom co-founded Sense Worldwide prior to joining The Future Laboratory in 2005, where his team conducts trend research and brand strategy for the likes of Nokia, BMW, Lamborghini and Coke Zero. Tom has also taught fashion textile students at the University of Brighton and University of East London.

He is passionate about understanding the emotional aspects of consumer behaviour and enabling brands to express their personality.

Jess Search

**Chief Executive
Channel 4 BRITDOC Foundation**

Jess is the chief executive of the Channel 4 BRITDOC Foundation (britdoc.org). The foundation is five years old and has supported more than 50 films including this year's Sundance double winner Afghan Star, Grierson winner Here's Johnny, and Chosen, which has been nominated for a BAFTA.

Jess is now working on a part-time MBA at Cass Business School and remains involved in shootingpeople.org, the online filmmakers' network she founded, which celebrated its 10th birthday last year with 38,000 members.

Stuart Semple

Artist

Stuart Semple is a leading British artist who has exhibited worldwide; his painterly critiques of mass culture having won him much critical acclaim. Stuart has collaborated with major brands including Levi's, Selfridges, Moncler and band The Prodigy. His works are owned by Debbie Harry, Dhani Harrison and Sienna Miller, among others.

Stuart writes for Art of England magazine and is a member of DACS Creators' Council. He lives and works in London and Dorset.

'It's impossible to define cool, but different factors resonate at different times. I think at the moment we're all fed up with being fed up, so something that makes me smile – I'm not saying laugh out loud – goes down well. I'd score that highly.'

Lauretta Roberts
Digital Development Director, WGSN

Michael Acton Smith

CEO
Mind Candy

Michael founded the online games company Mind Candy and also co-founded the online retailer Firebox.com 10 years ago in a Cardiff attic with £1,000.

He also created Moshi Monsters – the online world of adoptable pet monsters – and invented the Shot Glass Chess Set, a best-selling fusion of chess and alcohol.

In 2004, Michael created Perplex City, a global treasure hunt with a £100,000 prize.

Roger Wade

Director
Brands Incorporated

Roger runs his own brand consultancy, Brands Incorporated, specialising in licensing and raising finance for UK fashion brands. He works with major British brands such as Superdry, Bench, Ringspun, Religion, Richard James, Katharine Hamnett and Timothy Everest. In 1989, he founded the original British streetwear brand Boxfresh, and was the first to import Carhartt and G-Star into the UK.

Roger is a regular columnist for Drapers magazine, and a speaker at London and Manchester Fashion Networks.

Stephen Cheliotis

Chairman, Superbrands Councils UK & Chief Executive, The Centre for Brand Analysis

Stephen began his career at Brand Finance, advising companies on maximising shareholder value through brand management. He joined Superbrands in 2001, rising to UK managing director before moving on to a European role.

Stephen left Superbrands in 2008 to establish The Centre for Brand Analysis (TCBA). TCBA is contracted to run the CoolBrands selection process.

'Cool isn't about trying to be something, it's about being brave enough to externalise a quality that makes something truly unique. The more natural and effortless that process is, the cooler something becomes.'

Michael Acton Smith
CEO, Mind Candy

'Whether it's hip, stylish, chic, trendy, or up-to-the-minute, this book represents some of the coolest brands in the UK.'

Roger Wade
Director, Brands Incorporated

CoolBrands® Book

The small impressive agency with big impressive clients, August Media works its refreshingly different approach to customer publishing to deliver outstanding magazines and digital content for some of the UK's best-loved brands.

Founded in 2005 by some of consumer magazines' brightest stars, August Media is a feisty young agency whose success stems from a blend of professionalism, decades of experience, keen talent and a consuming passion for creative content. It's recognised as a different sort of agency from the mainstream because it thinks differently: more creatively, more astutely, more imaginatively. And it's this approach that made August the ideal choice for this year's CoolBrands publication. There was a buzz of excitement within the agency about working on the project and a real 'hands-up' moment when they asked who wanted to be involved.

For CoolBrands 2009/10, August Media's designers and editors worked closely with Superbrands UK to ensure that each brand is showcased in a clean, modern design that lets its unique identity shine through.

augustmedia.com

CoolBrands® digital

The 2009/10 programme sees the launch of CoolBrands® digital – a new, online presence that helps bring the brands featured in this book to life – to find out more visit CoolBrandsDigital.com.

Built on Ceros – a digital publishing platform – CoolBrands digital allows each brand to express its personality using a combination of video, animation and interactivity. Each CoolBrands digital entry also features a brand synopsis, striking imagery and a direct link to each brand's own website.

CoolBrands digital has been launched to enable brand-owners to reach a wide audience without the need for publishing an excessive number of books. This is a reflection of the environmental policies of many brands featured in the 2009/10 programme. The new, digital platform also follows the publisher's decision in 2007 to use only FSC-certified papers and vegetable-based dyes and inks in the production of all CoolBrands publications and associated materials.

CoolBrandsDigital.com

Qualifying CoolBrands® 2009/10

- A.P.C.
- Abel & Cole
- Absolut
- Acne Jeans
- Adidas
- AGA
- Agent Provocateur
- Alessi
- Alexander McQueen
- Alfa Romeo
- All Saints
- Amazon.co.uk
- American Apparel
- Anna Sui
- Anya Hindmarch
- Apple
- Aprilia
- Artisan Du Chocolat
- Asia de Cuba
- Asos.com
- Aston Martin
- Atari
- Audi
- Aussie
- Aveda
- B&B Italia
- Balenciaga
- Baltic
- Bang & Olufsen
- Barbican Centre
- Barbour
- Basilico
- BBC
- BBC iPlayer
- Bebo
- Beck's
- Belvedere Vodka
- Belvoir Cordials
- Ben & Jerry's
- Benefit
- Bentley
- Berghaus
- Beyond Retro
- Beyond the Valley
- BFI Southbank
- Billabong
- Birkenstock

- Bisque
- BlackBerry
- Blaupunkt
- Bliss
- BMW
- Bobbi Brown
- Boffi
- Bollinger
- Bombay Sapphire
- Botanics
- Bowers & Wilkins
- Brabantia
- British Airways
- British Museum
- Browns
- BSA
- Buddhistpunk
- Budweiser Budvar
- Buell
- Bulthaup
- Bumble and bumble
- Burberry
- Burton
- Burt's Bees
- Burts Potato Chips
- Busaba Eathai
- Cambridge Audio
- Canon
- Carluccio's
- Cath Kidston
- Chanel
- Channel 4
- Chantecaille
- Chivas Regal
- Chloé
- Christian Louboutin
- Cirque du Soleil
- Citizens of Humanity
- Clarins
- Clinique
- Cobra
- Coca-Cola
- Comme des Garçons
- Connect4
- Converse All Stars
- Corona
- Courvoisier

- Crème de la Mer
- Crooked Tongues
- Darphin
- Dave
- Daylesford Organic
- Dazed & Confused
- Decléor
- De'Longhi
- Denon
- Dermalogica
- Descamps
- Design Hotels
- Design Museum
- Diesel
- Diptyque
- Disaronno
- Divine
- Dolce V
- Dom Pérignon
- Dorset Cereals
- Dr Martens
- Dr Sebagh
- Dr.Hauschka
- Drakes
- Dries Van Noten
- Ducati
- E&O
- EA
- Eat.
- EBay
- Eden Project
- Edun
- Egg
- Elemis
- Elle Macpherson Intimates
- Emporio Armani
- Espa
- Estée Lauder
- Eurostar
- Eve Lom
- Evian
- Expedia
- FA Premier League
- Facebook
- Farrow & Ball
- Ferrari

- Fever-Tree
- Fiat 500
- First Direct
- Flickr
- Fortnum & Mason
- Foster + Partners
- Fred Perry
- Fudge
- Fuji
- Gaggenau
- Gaggia
- Gaydar.co.uk
- Georgina Goodman
- Ghd
- Ghost
- Gio-Goi
- Givenchy
- Glacéau Vitaminwater
- Glenfiddich
- Global Knives
- Globe-Trotter
- Google
- Gourmet Burger Kitchen
- GQ
- Graham & Green
- Green & Black's
- Grey Goose
- Grolsch
- G-Star Raw
- Gü
- Gucci
- Guerlain
- Guinness
- Guitar Hero
- H&M
- Häagen-Dazs
- Habitat
- Hakkasan
- Hamleys
- Harley-Davidson
- Harman Kardon
- Harrods
- Harvey Nichols
- Havaianas
- Havana Club

- Heal's
- Helly Hansen
- Hendricks
- Hennessy
- HMV
- Hoegaarden
- Hornby
- Hotel Chocolat
- Hotel du Vin
- Howies
- Hoxton Hotel
- ICA
- Iittala
- Ikea
- Illy
- Innocent
- IPhone
- IPod
- Issey Miyake
- Itsu
- Jack Daniel's
- Jaguar
- James Brown London
- Jean Paul Gaultier
- Jelly Belly
- Jimmy Choo
- Jo Malone
- John Frieda
- John Smedley
- Juice Republic
- Kawasaki
- KEF
- Kéraskin Esthetics
- Kérastase
- Kettle Chips
- Kiehl's
- King of Shaves
- Kiss
- KitchenAid
- Konami
- Korres
- Krug
- Krups
- Kurt Geiger
- La Perla
- La Prairie

- Lacoste
- Lamborghini
- Lancôme
- Land Rover
- Lara Bohinc
- L'Artisan Parfumeur
- Last.fm
- Lastminute.com
- Laura Mercier
- Laurent-Perrier
- Lavazza
- Le Creuset
- Leatherman
- Lee Jeans
- Leffe
- Leica
- Levi Roots
- Levi's
- Lexus
- LG
- Liberty
- Ligne Roset
- Lindt
- Linn
- Locanda Locatelli
- L'Occitane en Provence
- Loewe
- London 2012
- London Eye
- Lonely Planet
- L'Oréal
- Lotus
- Louis Vuitton
- Lovefilm
- Lulu Guinness
- Lyle & Scott
- M.A.C
- Madame V
- Maglite
- Magners
- Malmaison
- Mandarina Duck
- Manolo Blahnik
- Marc Jacobs
- Marks & Spencer
- Marmite

- Marni
- Marshall
- Matthew Williamson
- McLaren F1
- Mercedes-Benz
- Miele
- Millennium Stadium
- Mini
- Modern Toss
- Möet & Chandon
- Montezuma's
- Mr & Mrs Smith
- MTV
- Muji
- Myla
- MySpace
- Nails Inc.
- Narciso Rodriguez
- Nars
- National Geographic
- Neal's Yard Dairy
- Neal's Yard Remedies
- Neff
- Net-A-Porter
- New Balance
- New Covent Garden Food Co.
- New York Bagel Company
- Nicholas Kirkwood
- Nike
- Nikon
- Nintendo
- Nobu
- Nokia
- Nude Skincare
- Nudie Jeans
- O2
- Oakley
- Olympus
- Onitsuka Tiger
- Orange
- Origins
- Paint & Paper Library
- Patagonia

- Paul Smith
- Pentax
- Peroni Nastro Azzurro
- Perrier
- Philips
- Phyto
- Piaggio
- Pimm's
- Planet Organic
- Play.com
- PlayStation
- Poggenpohl
- Porsche
- Poste Mistress
- PPQ
- Prada
- Prescriptives
- Pret A Manger
- Proud Galleries
- Puma
- Pure
- Quiksilver
- Rachel's Organic
- Raleigh
- Ralph Lauren
- Ray-Ban
- Raymond Weil
- Red Wing
- Reebok
- Rémy Martin
- Ren
- Richard Rogers
- Rigby & Peller
- Rimmel London
- Rip Curl
- Roberto Cavalli
- Roberts Radio
- Roc
- Rock & Republic
- Rococo Chocolates
- Roka
- Roland
- Rolex
- Rolls-Royce
- Rough Guides
- Rough Trade Shops

- Roundhouse
- Royal Albert Hall
- Royal Opera House
- Rubik's Cube
- Russian Standard Vodka
- S. Pellegrino
- Saab
- Saatchi Gallery
- Salty Dog Crisps
- Samsonite
- Samsung
- San Miguel
- Sanderson
- Scalextric
- Scooterman
- Scott's
- Scrabble
- Seeds of Change
- Sega
- Select Models
- Selfridges
- Sennheiser
- Shiseido
- Shoreditch House
- Sketch
- SK-II
- Skinny Cow
- Sky
- Sky+
- Skylon
- Skype
- Smart Car
- Smeg
- Smirnoff
- Smythson of Bond Street
- Sony
- Sony Ericsson
- Southbank Centre
- Space Nk
- Specialized
- Square Pie
- St Martins Lane
- St. Tropez
- STA Travel
- Staropramen

- Start
- Stella Artois
- Stella McCartney
- Stephen Webster
- Stila
- Stolichnaya
- Storm
- Streetcar
- Superdry
- Swarovski
- Swatch
- Tag Heuer
- Talisker
- Tanner Krolle
- Tanqueray gin
- Tate Modern
- Terry de Havilland
- The Cinnamon Club
- The Connaught
- The Conran Shop
- The Co-operative Bank
- The Fat Duck
- The Glenlivet
- The Guardian
- The Ivy
- The Lowry
- The North Face
- The O2
- The Observer
- The Old Vic
- The Organic Pharmacy
- The Rivington
- The Sanctuary
- The Times
- The Wapping Project
- The White Company
- The Wolseley
- The Zetter
- Thecoolhunter.co.uk
- Thierry Mugler
- Tiffany & Co.
- Tiger Beer
- Time Out City Guides
- Tom Ford

- TomTom
- Toni&Guy
- Top Trumps
- Topman
- Topshop
- Trailfinders
- Tresemmé
- Trish McEvoy
- Triumph
- Twitter
- Tyrrells
- Uniqlo
- Urban Outfitters
- Urban Splash
- V&A
- Vaio
- Vans
- Vespa
- Veuve Clicquot
- Villeroy & Boch
- Virgin Atlantic
- Virgin Money
- Vitra
- Vivienne Westwood
- Vogue
- VV Rouleaux
- VW Beetle
- Wagamama
- Wahaca
- Waitrose
- Wallpaper* City Guides
- Wembley Stadium
- Whole Foods Market
- Williams F1
- Wimbledon Championship
- Wolford
- Xbox
- Yamaha
- Yauatcha
- YMC
- YO! Sushi
- YouTube
- YSL
- Zara
- Zopa